DEATH'S JEST-BOOK

THOMAS LOVELL BEDDOES (1803–1849) was born in Clifton in Bristol, the son of the renowned scientist and radical Thomas Beddoes and Anna, sister of the novelist Maria Edgeworth. He published *The Brides' Tragedy* (1822) to critical acclaim while still an undergraduate student at Oxford. Encouraged by this early success, he aspired to fame as a poet and dramatist: his passion for Shakespeare and early modern drama led him to draft several new tragedies in the Elizabethan / Jacobean style, which now exist only as collections of fragments. In his reading of modern writers, Beddoes was a devout admirer of Shelley, assisting with the publication of his *Posthumous Poems* (1824). In 1825 Beddoes committed himself to the study of medicine, travelling to Germany, where he enrolled at the University of Göttingen. At the same time as embarking on his medical studies, he began to write the text that was to become a lifelong obsession – *Death's Jest-Book*. Beddoes had an uneven medical career, complicated at times by his involvement in radical political movements: he travelled widely, settling in various university cities in Germany and Switzerland. He frequently fell prey to depression; and became increasingly isolated from friends and family in England, claiming to be more at home in German than in his native language. Beddoes never published *Death's Jest-Book* in his lifetime, but continued to revise and expand it right up until his death by suicide in 1849. Beddoes's work has never enjoyed unequivocal fame, but he is now widely recognised as one of the most intense and challenging of late Romantic voices.

MICHAEL BRADSHAW is a lecturer in English at the Manchester Metropolitan University; he is the author of *Resurrection Songs: The Poetry of Thomas Lovell Beddoes*, and co-editor of Beddoes's *Selected Poetry*; he has also published on George Darley, John Keats and Mary Shelley.

Fyfield*Books* aim to make available some of the great classics of British and European literature in clear, affordable formats, and to restore often neglected writers to their place in literary tradition.

Fyfield*Books* take their name from the Fyfield elm in Matthew Arnold's 'Scholar Gypsy' and 'Thyrsis'. The tree stood not far from the village where the series was originally devised in 1971.

> *Roam on! The light we sought is shining still.*
> *Dost thou ask proof? Our tree yet crowns the hill,*
> *Our Scholar travels yet the loved hill-side*

from 'Thyrsis'

THOMAS LOVELL BEDDOES

Death's Jest-Book
The 1829 text

Edited with an introduction by
MICHAEL BRADSHAW

FyfieldBooks

CARCANET

in association with
the Thomas Lovell Beddoes Society

First published in Great Britain in 2003 by
Carcanet Press Limited
Alliance House
Cross Street
Manchester M2 7AQ
in association with the Thomas Lovell Beddoes Society

A CIP catalogue record for this book is available from the British Library
ISBN 1 85754 599 0

The publisher acknowledges financial assistance from
Arts Council England

Typeset by XL Publishing Services, Tiverton

In memory of
Ron Beddoes
and
Dorothy Clarkson

ACKNOWLEDGEMENTS

The editor and publishers gratefully acknowledge the permission of Taylor & Francis Books to use the β text of *Death's Jest-Book* from H.W. Donner's *The Works of Thomas Lovell Beddoes* (Oxford: Oxford University Press, 1935) as the copy text of this edition.

My thanks are due to Laura Ellis for her invaluable help with proof-reading. I am grateful for the support of colleagues at Carcanet and Manchester Metropolitan University – Michael Schmidt, Judith Willson, Jeffrey Wainwright, Barry Atkins and Simon Malpas; and also to colleagues in the Beddoes Society – Judith Higgens, Ute Berns and Shelley Rees. And special thanks as ever to my family: Desdemona, Jacob and Ruby.

This is the first complete edition of *Death's Jest-Book* to be published for twenty-five years, and the first ever book to make this extraordinary text available to a wider range of readers, scholars and students as an affordable paperback. We are indebted to the Thomas Lovell Beddoes Society, and especially to its dedicated chairman, John Lovell Beddoes, not only for assistance with the publication of this edition, but more generally for raising the profile of the poet over the past decade. Contact details for the Society can be found at the end of this book.

CONTENTS

INTRODUCTION

Thomas Lovell Beddoes was an exceptional poet, and *Death's Jest-Book* is his defining text, a pastiche Renaissance tragedy replete with treachery, murder, sorcery and haunting, the extravagant expression of the poet's lifelong obsession with mortality and immortality. It is a classic of the literature of death. The text contains some of the most powerful blank verse by any of the British Romantics, and is surely among the most intense of Romantic dramas, but has never been properly absorbed into the Romantic canon. *Death's Jest-Book* is rich in self-contradiction: a text which aims to marry despair and 'wildest mirth'; a work of late Romanticism wholly in love with the poetry and drama of the Renaissance; written with a deep critical knowledge of the European theatre and yet long considered unperformable as a play; the work of a neglected minor author, who nevertheless can count Browning, Gosse, Pound, Ashbery and Ricks among his many admirers.

Beddoes lived and wrote at the very end of what we now know as the Romantic period. His first major publication, *The Improvisatore* (1821), was published in the year of Keats's death; his second, and only successful publication, *The Brides' Tragedy* (1822) was published in the year of Shelley's death; Byron lived a couple more years. With the odd hindsight of literary 'periodisation' readers have always found it hard to account for Beddoes in terms of his own time – just too late to be a true Romantic, and too early for a fully fledged Victorian, Beddoes seems to inhabit a lost generation of English writers. Certainly in his own reflections on the literary scene of his day, Beddoes is sardonic and unsparing of himself and his peers alike, and often brooded over the death of Shelley, which he felt had left everyone in the dark, bereft of direction.

The poet's father was the celebrated scientist and democrat Dr Thomas Beddoes (1760–1808), the friend of Coleridge and mentor of Humphry Davy. Having resigned from his position at Oxford due to hostility to his overt sympathy with the French Revolution, Thomas Beddoes founded the Pneumatic Institute in Bristol, a progressive centre for medical and chemical experimentation, specialising in the inhalation of gases or 'factitious airs'. A controversial and much revered figure, Dr Beddoes is thought to have instructed the young Thomas Lovell and his siblings with demonstrations of morbid anatomy. The poet's family on his mother's side was equally colourful; he was the nephew of the novelist Maria Edgeworth, and grandson of the radical educationalist and inventor Richard Lovell Edgeworth. At school and university, Thomas Lovell was both gifted and subversive; he quickly developed a taste for the extravagant and macabre in literature, and wrote some spirited 'Terror School' juvenilia. For a short while following the remarkable success of *The Brides' Tragedy*, Beddoes aspired to fame as a professional poet, but then made a firm commitment to the study and practice of medicine: in the summer of 1825, one of the watershed moments of his life, Beddoes travelled to Germany and enrolled in the University of Göttingen. At the same time as this, he began work on *Death's Jest-Book*, the fantastical dramatic experiment that was to occupy his literary talent for the rest of his life. The rejection of the completed manuscript of the drama by two of his friends was perhaps the defining crisis in both the life and works; it will be discussed further below. The perceived failure of the drama contributed to Beddoes's increasing depression; after a suicide attempt and some drunken escapades, he was expelled from the university in 1829. His next residence, at Würzburg, ended in expulsion from Bavaria in 1832 for his involvement with radical political groups. Beddoes then travelled to Switzerland, where he joined a growing community of political exiles and liberal intellectuals; he continued to study and practise medicine, and drafted new poetry, notably a long collection of tales and lyrics called *The Ivory Gate* that was to include the never-ending *Jest-Book*. Beddoes led an increasingly isolated and unsettled life, making occasional visits to England, where his friends and family found him difficult and irascible. In Basel in 1848 Beddoes attempted suicide by opening an artery in his left leg; he survived, but the leg was later amputated. In January 1849 he succeeded in killing himself, with poison. *Death's Jest-Book* was published the following year.

This is not a selected edition of an author, but a complete edition of one exceptional work; and we are primarily interested not in the history of Beddoes as such, but in the history of *Death's Jest-Book*. Fuller and more wide-ranging accounts of the life, works, evaluation and reputation of Thomas Lovell Beddoes are available elsewhere.[1] Instead, this introduction will deal primarily with the *Jest-Book* itself – its inception, its style, its history and transmission, and certain key critical responses.

Death's Jest-Book was partly the offspring of Beddoes's literary precocity and ambition. In 1822, at the age of just nineteen, Beddoes had published his first five-act drama, *The Brides' Tragedy*. In the following year it received extremely complimentary reviews: between them, George Darley (writing in *The London Magazine*), Bryan Waller Procter (*The London* and *The Edinburgh Review*) and John Wilson (*Blackwood's*) effectively identified Beddoes as the next major dramatist of his day, holding the young poet up as an example for others to follow, and looking ahead to years of spectacularly fulfilled promise. In 1823 and '24 Beddoes wrote confidently and fast, working on three new tragedies, *The Last Man*, *Love's Arrow Poisoned* and *The Second Brother*, which now exist as fragments of varying sizes. Young and talented, always highly opinionated, and now fired up by such extravagant praise, Beddoes showed considerable authority in his assessment of contemporary drama, in a letter of January 1825:

> Say what you will — I am convinced the man who is to awaken the drama must be a bold trampling fellow — no creeper into worm-holes — no reviser even — however good. These reanimations are vampire-cold. Such ghosts as Marloe, Webster &c are better dramatists, better poets, I dare say, than any contemporary of ours — but they are ghosts — the worm is in their pages — & we want to see something that our great-grandsires did not know. With the greatest reverence for all the antiquities of the drama, I still think that we had better beget than revive — attempt to give the literature of this age an idiosyncracy & spirit of its own, & only raise a ghost to gaze on, not to live with — just now the drama is a haunted ruin. (p. 595)[2]

Here, in one of his best-remembered statements on tragedy, Beddoes aptly summarises a stagnating contemporary taste for Elizabethan pastiche, and distances himself from it. And yet, coming from the author of *The Brides' Tragedy* and *The Second Brother*, the complaint seems to involve a measure of self-accusation: by this time Beddoes had published, and was once more in the process of writing, five-act blank verse tragedies in the Elizabethan / Jacobean style. But what might be said to distinguish his dramas from contemporaries in this revival genre is his self-directed irony; certainly in the richly satirical *Jest-Book*, but even in the early *Brides' Tragedy*, there is no complacent acceptance of the early modern form, but a questioning dialogue with earlier styles that Beddoes typically expresses in his skilful use of controlled anachronism. Beddoes is aware, painfully so in many of his confessional letters, of his failure to renew the poetic drama and set it alight once more. Tropes of grave-robbing, dismemberment, haunting and galvanism reverberate through his many accounts of his writing process (and still continue today in postmodern critical interpretations).

Beddoes seems to have conceived and begun *Death's Jest-Book* in the summer of 1825, at roughly the same time as he embarked for the German states to begin his medical training at the University of Göttingen. In June he wrote from Oxford to his friend, later to be his literary executor, Thomas Forbes Kelsall, with his first announcement of the new tragedy:

> I do not intend to finish that 2nd Brother you saw but am thinking of a very Gothic-styled tragedy, for w^h I have a very jewel of a name —
> DEATH'S JESTBOOK — of course no one will ever read it — Mr. Milman (our poetry professor) has made me quite unfashionable here, by denouncing me, as one of a 'villainous school'. (p. 604)

Clearly proud of and excited by the title he has hit upon, Beddoes is also apparently encouraged by the disapproval of authority figures such as Henry Hart Milman. He is noticeably cheerful as he reflects on the likelihood that no one will read the new drama: this ironic attitude to the prospects of publication, readership and fame were to grow steadily graver and more intense throughout the next two decades. In July 1825 Beddoes travelled to Germany and began his studies at Göttingen; we next hear of the *Jest-Book* in December, when he writes to Kelsall, excusing his recent lack of correspondence by detailing the industries of his average working day:

> Up at 5, Anatomical reading till 6 — translation from English into German till 7 — Prepare for Blumenbach's lecture till 9 — Stromeyer's lecture on Chemistry till 10. 10 to ½ p. 12, Practical Zootomy — ½ p. 12 to 1 English into German or German literary reading with a pipe — 1 to 2 Anatomical lecture. 2 to 3

anatomical reading. 3 to 4 Osteology. 4 to 5 Lecture in German language. 5 to 6 dinner and *light* reading in Zootomy, Chem. or Anat^y. 6 to 7, this hour is very often wasted in a visit, sometimes Anatomical reading till 8. Then coffee and read Greek till 10. 10 to 11, write a little Death's Jest book w^h is a horrible waste of time, but one must now & then throw away the dregs of the day; read Latin sometimes or even continue the Anatomy — and at 11 go to bed. (pp. 608–9)

The writing of the momentous *Jest-Book* is dismissed over-casually, in a throwaway style that probably didn't fool Kelsall for a minute; ironic self-defence is a persistent feature of Beddoes's comedy. Yet even if he were trying to diminish its relative importance, it is interesting how Beddoes situates his drama here – embedded in and surrounded by a thick concentration of linguistic and biological studies. And among these Beddoes gives special weight to the anatomical. In the following passage from the same letter, Beddoes reinforces this connection between his scientific and poetic ambitions:

Again, even as a dramatist, I cannot help thinking that the study of anat^y, physiol-, psych-, & anthropol-ogy applied to and illustrated by history, biography and works of imagination is that w^h is most likely to assist one in producing correct and masterly delineations of the passions: great light w^d be t hrown on Shakespeare by the commentaries of a person so educated. The studies then of the dramatist & physician are closely, almost inseparably, allied; the application alone is different; but is it impossible for the same man to combine these two professions, in some degree at least? The science of psychology, mental varieties, has long been used by physicians, in conjunction with the corresponding corporeal knowledge, for the investigation & removal of immaterial causes of disease; it still remains for some one to exhibit the sum of his experience in mental pathology & therapeutics, not in a cold technical dead description, but a living semiotical display, a series of anthropological experiments, developed for the purpose of ascertaining some important psychical principle — i.e. a tragedy. Thus far to show you that my studies, pursued as I pledge myself to pursue them, are not hostile, but rather favourable to the development of a germ w^h I w^d fain believe within me. (p. 609)

Far from being merely the poet's latest attempt at tragic theatre, *Death's Jest-Book* was clearly assuming a privileged status in his imagination, transcending the journeyman-work of 1822 to '24. *Death's Jest-Book* is presented now as an experimental fusing of arts and sciences. And in that last sentence, Beddoes offers a personal reassurance to Kelsall, who more than anyone encouraged and supported him with belief in the importance of his literary talent, that medicine was not claiming him away from poetry; on the contrary, he argues, the medical and the poetic have become mutually sustaining, co-operating towards a higher synthesis. In these heady early days of the *Jest-Book*, Beddoes shows himself to be full of cheerful cussedness and impetuous confidence:

> Death's Jest-book goes on like the tortoise — slow & sure; I think it will be entertaining, very unamiable, & utterly unpopular. (p. 610)

> Apollo has been barbarously separated by the moderns: I would endeavour to unite him. (p. 611)

But all these boasts are rather general: apart from fusing the medical and the literary in a psychological enquiry, apart from getting up the nose of the complacent English reader, what was *Death's Jest-Book* really *about*? What did it contain? It was in a verse letter to his friend the poet Bryan Waller Procter ('Barry Cornwall') in March 1826, that Beddoes gave the most spirited and startling account of the genesis of his new tragedy, and formally announced its theme:

>   ... I have been
> Giving some negro minutes of the night
> Freed from the slavery of my ruling spright
> Anatomy the grim, to a new story
> In whose satiric pathos we will glory.
> In it Despair has married wildest Mirth
> And to their wedding-banquet all the earth
> Is bade to bring its enmities and loves
> Triumphs and horrors: you shall see the doves
> Billing with quiet joy and all the while
> Their nests's the scull of some old king of Nile:
> But he who fills the cup and makes the jest
> Pipes to the dancers, is the fool o' the feast.
> Who's he? I've dug him up and decked him trim

And made a mock, a fool, a slave of him
Who was the planet's tyrant: dotard death:
Man's hate and dread: not with a stoical breath
To meet him like Augustus standing up,
Nor with grave saws to season the cold cup
Like the philosopher nor yet to hail
His coming with a verse or jesting tale
As Adrian did and More: but of his night
His moony ghostliness and silent might
To rob him, to un-cypress him i' the light
To unmask all his secrets; make him play
Momus o'er wine by torchlight is the way
To conquer him and kill; and from the day
Spurned hissed and hooted send him back again
An unmasked braggart to his bankrupt den.
For death is more 'a jest' than Life: you see
Contempt grows quick from familiarity.
I owe this wisdom to Anatomy — (pp. 614–15)

The writing of the tragedy is described as a furtive nocturnal labour, a rival to the claims of his legitimate study of anatomy, and yet also closely related to it in its morbid fixation and its attempt to unmask and expose. With repeated images of stripping down, Beddoes self-consciously adapts the methods of the dissecting room to his satirical mission to expose the fraudulence of human death. Death is to play Momus, 'the fool o' the feast'. Both the writer and the original reader of this letter were fully aware of the structural irony here: when we create a fool for our own amusement, his commission may lead him to redirect the laughter at us. Fools are double, unstable creatures, who love to backfire on their creators. Sure enough, when the clown Mandrake emerges from the tomb in Act III, Scene iii, believing himself to have died and risen again, he speaks a direct parody of this rash statement of ambition by Beddoes: death is a minor hiccup, and we have been needlessly living in fear; Mandrake will expose death for a fraud by recording his experiences in published essays. In the verse letter, one could argue, Beddoes is noisily courting disaster, marking out the inevitability of his failure; in Mandrake's 'resurrection' Beddoes delivers the punchline. Self-defeat, and the sardonic embrace of defeat, are hardwired into this drama from the outset: the failure to unmask death, the failure to resurrect the

Muse of tragedy, the failure to unite the two aspects of Apollo, the failure to achieve a theatre of the human psychology – all are amply dramatised by this most self-reflexive of texts. But as the tragedy of its own tragic theme, as an ironic investigation into human obsession and self-deception, *Death's Jest-Book* is a magnificent challenge to the modern reader; and in the fascinating intricacy of its writing in verse and prose, *Death's Jest-Book* is a thrilling success.

Death's Jest-Book is a revenge tragedy. The plot concerns two brothers who have sworn revenge on the corrupt Duke of Münsterberg, Melveric. They are Wolfram, a generous and heroic knight who gives up his search for vengeance and befriends the Duke, and Isbrand, disguised as a jester, who nurses his sense of grievance and becomes an obsessive and sadistic revenger in the classic Jacobean style. The Duke has been taken prisoner on a crusade; Wolfram makes an expedition to rescue him from captivity, and saves his life; but by this time the two friends have become rivals for the love of Sibylla, and once freed the Duke murders Wolfram at the end of Act I. When Wolfram's body is shipped home, Isbrand smuggles it into the vault in which the Duke's wife is buried, there to lie in wait for him, a shock accusation on Judgement Day; the clown Mandrake has also hidden in this tomb. Isbrand has joined the Duke's two sons, Adalmar and Athulf, in a conspiracy to overthrow the Duke: disguised, the Duke joins the conspirators in their nocturnal carousing. Later, the Duke uses his necromant slave to try and raise his wife from the dead, but of course doesn't get what he expected: first Mandrake appears, with some fine comic speeches, and then the risen ghost of Wolfram, to plague Melveric with his own guilt. This long scene of resurrection takes place in a ruined cathedral decorated with a 'Dance of Death' frieze. The rest of the plot concerns the rise and fall of Isbrand as a replacement tyrant; the conflict between the two princes, also rivals in love; and the 'wooing' of Sibylla by the ghost. Isbrand is summarily executed by Mario, a symbolic character devoted to Liberty; in the final lines of the drama, the Duke is led off 'still alive, into the world o' th' dead' by Wolfram.

As previously with *The Brides' Tragedy*, Beddoes's considerable knowledge of Elizabethan and Jacobean theatre is in evidence throughout, but *Death's Jest-Book* has often been treated unfairly as an exercise in hollow pastiche or revivalism. Beddoes is expert at ironic anachronism, for example in the way he conflates the Renaissance revenge plot with a nineteenth-century sense of popular revolution. But the use of historical time is even more complex than this: the dramatic setting achieves a surprisingly plausible 'mediaevalism', especially in the use of feudal and chivalric motifs in Act I. In fact Beddoes is juggling three different historical periods, to give the drama a multi-layered sense of theatrical time.

Critics have long troubled over questions of period and genre in the *Jest-Book*, but none perhaps have quite done justice to the complexity and self-consciousness of Beddoes's experiment.³ As shown in the letter about 'vampire-cold' revivals of Renaissance drama, Beddoes was both informed and opinionated on questions of theatrical method and taste. Beddoes's Preface to *Death's Jest-Book*, printed here alongside the text, is an interesting document: among the many tortured sentences and gratuitous bardolatry, Beddoes makes an intelligible case for the preservation of a native theatre, and against the importation of classical criteria against which to judge it. The sustained analogy between a tragedy in the English style and a Gothic cathedral, which Beddoes has adapted from A.W. Schlegel, is made concrete in Acts III and V of his own *Tragedy*, in which key scenes are set among cathedral ruins decorated with a frieze of the Dance of Death. It is important to recall the Preface at these moments in the drama, in order to understand Beddoes's critical and meta-theatrical point, that the contemporary incarnation of tragedy only survives by turning inward, repeating its own forms in a beleaguered attempt to preserve a sense of the sacred. In the final paragraph of the Preface Beddoes threatens to write an anonymous review damning his own performance, slurring himself with allegations of plagiarism and predictably touting the élitist classical values. It is surely significant that for all Beddoes's ambition to produce a 'medical' form of drama, and to dramatise certain scientific precepts, it is with his complaints about the theatre and swipes at vain reviewers that he envisaged confronting his first readers.

But quite apart from his familiarity with the early modern stage, in the early *Jest-Book* Beddoes is managing a whole variety of sources. The medical precepts outlined in the letters have certainly filtered through into the language of the drama, particularly in moments of detailed visual imagery. When, for example, Isbrand describes a lance as 'A delicate tool to breathe a heathen's vein with' (II.iii.68), he is speaking the language of the dissecting room, a thrilling glimpse of the warrior as surgeon, or experimental anatomist. Condemning his brother for his change of heart, Isbrand asks him, 'Say when hast thou undergone transfusion, and whose hostile blood now turns thy life's wheels?' (I.i.159–61), Beddoes testing out his imaginative connection between moral psychology and physiology. And in the Duke's melancholy reflections on the precariousness of life, we see Beddoes again experimenting with scientific imagery, this time with the idea of microscopic organisms:

> If man could see
> The perils and diseases that he elbows,
> Each day he walks a mile; which catch at him,
> Which fall behind and graze him as he passes;
> Then would he know that Life's a single pilgrim,
> Fighting unarmed amongst a thousand soldiers. (IV.i.9–14)

Similarly, if the clown Mandrake prattles of Paracelsus and the philosopher's stone, as he embarks for his escapade in Egypt, (I.i.23–32), Beddoes was actually steeped in alchemical reading as he drafted these scenes and prepared them for the press. Mandrake's title is of course Homunculus; and he refers to his being in the service of an unseen, off-stage 'Doctor' (I.i.6–8), who may or may not be Paracelsus himself.[4] Mandrake's alchemical subplot is farcical in style, and yet indicates the presence of an important mystical strand in Beddoes's multi-layered experiment.

Some of Beddoes's characteristic irony as a poet and dramatist, as he balances these various themes and sources against each other, can be demonstrated in a brief quotation from one of Isbrand's speeches from Act III:

> 'Neath Grüssau's tiles sleep none, whose deepest bosom
> My fathom hath not measured; none, whose thoughts
> I have not made a map of. In the depth
> And labyrinthine home of the still soul,
> Where the seen thing is imaged, and the whisper
> Joints the expecting spirit, my spies, which are
> Suspicion's creeping words, have stolen in,
> And, with their eyed feelers, touched and sounded
> The little hiding holes of cunning thought,
> And each dark crack in which a reptile purpose

Hangs in its chrysalis unripe for birth.
All of each heart I know. (III.iii.77–88)

In a speech like this, we can observe a collision of several of the themes which excited and motivated Beddoes as a writer – treachery, anatomy, psychology, violent revolution... Isbrand conveys the dissector's precise measurement of the textures and processes of the human body, but of course Beddoes is also representing this ethic of precise experimentation as neurotic and disturbed, drawing attention to the potential for abuse in Isbrand's fantasy of probing every individual mind. Münsterberg is imagined as a state in dire need of liberation, but also threatened by its overreaching liberator. Isbrand states that the agents who do this anatomising work for him are 'Suspicion's creeping words'; and this allusion to language illustrates another feature of Beddoes's trademark macabre. Dating back at least to the fragments of *The Last Man* (1823), Beddoes had drawn imaginative parallels between the text and the body – especially the murdered body and the body threatened by violence. Since 1825 the many accounts of the writing of the *Jest-Book* in Beddoes's letters to England had begun to develop a more explicit analogy between the erratic growth of the tragedy and the macabre human body, which is often imagined in a state of dismemberment. Directing a reader's attention to the relationship between words and bodies, Beddoes is reflecting on the complex, stitched-up textuality of his drama itself.

The drama was complete in its earliest form by the end of 1828. A fair copy was made, and then a special transcript for the press, which Beddoes despatched with eagerness (couched in tactical nonchalance) to his friends in England in February 1829. The manuscript was read by three trusted friends – Kelsall, Procter and J.G.H. Bourne. Kelsall later claimed to have reacted favourably to the text, and recommended publication.[5] But Procter and Bourne were negative and deeply disapproving, and advised Beddoes not to publish without root-and-branch revision; their letters do not survive, but are thought to have been strongly expressed. It is hard for a modern reader of Beddoes to forgive Procter in particular for this ungenerous and fatal intervention in Beddoes's growth as a writer, when Procter's own rather bland verse was so flattered and overvalued.[6] The sudden summary rejection of Beddoes's great poetic experiment was a moment of genuine crisis, contributing to a depression that led to his first suicide attempt, and changing permanently his attitude towards publication and readership.[7] This is a defining moment of Beddoes's writing career: with the publication of the *Jest-Book* indefinitely suspended, Beddoes began to write in a different way, and very soon left the 'satiric pathos' of *The Fool's Tragedy* far behind him. He expanded the text enormously, moving sharply away from the formal constraints of a tragic action. An abundance of lyrics was drafted for inclusion within the growing drama. The majority of new material Beddoes wrote in the 1830s and '40s had some association with the *Jest-Book*. When new volumes were planned (such as *Charonic Steps* and *The Ivory Gate*) they were intended not as entirely separate ventures, but as large-scale frames, new ways of presenting the *Jest-Book*. This long and uncertain programme of revision after 1829, but especially between 1838 and '44, Beddoes's editor H.W. Donner calls the γ text. This is another *Jest-Book* entirely, containing a fully revised Act I, greatly expanded with ironic lyrics, and a number of changes, insertions and deletions that represent Beddoes's unfinished attempt entirely to recast the drama in a new style.

There are continuing arguments over the respective intellectual and aesthetic merits of each version. What is certain is that they are distinct – as significantly different from each other as the texts of *King Lear*, or *The Prelude*. *Death's Jest-Book; or, The Fool's Tragedy* (1829) is a satirical tragedy, essentially obedient to the conventional five-act structure, centred on a revenge plot, and predominantly written in blank verse and prose. *Death's Jest-Book; or, The Day Will Come* (post-1829, but principally 1838–44) has developed far away from this origin, the tragic structure fading to the point of dissolution with the incorporation of nine new lyrics in the first act; the material stage play element has also waned in favour of a psychic 'theatre' of disembodied voices. Faced with a difficult choice between these two immensely different creations, I have opted for the earlier version. For the present edition I have chosen to use what I have called 'the 1829 text' (otherwise Donner's β text), essentially for the following three reasons.

Firstly, as far as it is possible to tell, this is the form in which the drama would have been published in Beddoes's lifetime, but for the negative advice of his friends.[8] Beddoes considered the drama finished in 1829; and it seems that he wanted to publish it in this form. The uneven programme of revision that followed in the 1830s and '40s is the creature of Procter's rejection, and Beddoes's suppression of this version. So the early text of *Death's Jest-Book* which is presented in this edition captures the drama at the very moment when Beddoes felt it was ready for consumption. We can only imagine the impact it might have had in England's poetic twilight of 1829: 'what if...?'

Secondly, in 1829 the *Jest-Book* is still a tragedy in form, and is still recognisable as the work Beddoes outlined in the great verse letter to Procter, the marriage of despair and mirth 'in whose satiric pathos we will glory'. A pretty long text even in this form, the early *Jest-Book* nevertheless has a bracing sense of purpose about it that the poet totally relinquished in his later ironic lyricism. The drama is subtitled a tragedy; and it is clear from many of the letters, as from the Preface, to whose argument Beddoes seems very committed, that the tragic was a vitally important part of its inception. The meta-dramatic satire in the Dance of Death scenes, the emphasis on the physicality of the resurrected Wolfram – features like these all suggest an interest in the materiality of performance that complicates the drama's received status as 'closet' or 'mental' theatre; and in 1829 this materiality is still present, and controlled by a coherent tragic structure.

The third and final reason is an extension of these: until early 1829 Beddoes was still studying avidly at Göttingen (he was expelled from the university in August), and the intensity of his studies has a fresh and direct influence on the drama. Although Beddoes continued to study and practise medicine throughout the later revisions of the *Jest-Book*, and also kept up his interest in the occult, he never seems to have recaptured the relentless energy and passion of the Göttingen years. Consequently the many anatomical allusions in the text have a special relationship with its early inception. In this way, the 1829 text of the drama is still close to some of its most distinctive sources, medical and alchemical; it retains a strong impression of Beddoes working to integrate their ideas and registers into his experimental tragedy, and gives us a flavour of those four driven years in Göttingen.

Critics of *Death's Jest-Book* have generally agreed that it is the central achievement of Beddoes's writing career. It is his great statement (for better and worse) on the mortality of the human, and the failed search for its immortality. Critical reaction to the drama has varied widely in theme and in temper: some critics lament its alleged formal disarray and cite it as an example of the declining Romantic vision, while others celebrate its wild intensity and ironic intelligence. The location of Beddoes in terms of literary periods has long been regarded as problematic, due both to his love-affair with the English Renaissance, and also to his 'transitional' generation, stranded somewhere between the 'Romantic' and the 'Victorian'. Lytton Strachey (1907) was an influential early critic who discussed the issue of Elizabethan pastiche in the *Jest-Book* and other works:[9] 'The Last Elizabethan' is a beautifully written and sympathetic assessment of Beddoes's talent, but attests to the inherent strangeness of a dramatic poetry which seems to live two hundred years in the past. In 'Beddoes and Chronology', Ezra Pound (1913) also considers the poet's archaic style, and the various literary-historical accidents which contribute to the making of an author.

For much of the twentieth century, Beddoes criticism and scholarship were overshadowed by H.W. Donner. Donner's critical biography *Thomas Lovell Beddoes: The Making of a Poet* (1935) established certain paradigms in the interpretation of *Death's Jest-Book* which have since proved enduring and slow to shift. It was Donner for instance who proposed the first substantial psychoanalytic argument, reading the drama as in part the literary exorcism of a death terror or 'skeleton complex'[10] that had its origin in the morbid dissections with which Dr Thomas Beddoes is thought to have educated his children. Donner also established the view that German 'Romantic irony' is of key importance in unlocking the hidden strategies of the text, a line since pursued by Anne Harrex (1967) and others. Donner devotes several major chapters to the *Jest-Book*, and constructs a narrative of its development: he records its inception as an ill-fated satire on death; he observes how this quickly gave way to a satire on human life, the skeleton complex neutralised by ironic detachment; and argues that it moved gradually towards a weary love of harmony, a longing for completion, the lyrical wish to die. Essentially, this is a tragic narrative, and in matching the works to the life, Donner is fully committed to the tragic structure and the tragic effect throughout. Some remarks from his 'Conclusion: An Aesthetic Summary' show how closely Donner associates the rhythms of the genre with the actual life history of his author:

Only when disharmony is dissolved in harmony and conflicting passions reconciled in a sublime atonement, do we experience the whole complexity that is contained in a perfect form. This seems to be the reason why tragedy has always been regarded as the highest form of art, for it admits us to witness that process of liberation which is the ideal of all human beings...[11]

In this commitment to an emotional theme, as well as in his habit of elevating the criterion of metrical euphony, Donner may now appear a conservative influence ripe to be discarded. Biographical criticism no longer enjoys such an unquestioned provenance. But much of Donner's argument seems to derive from his responsiveness to a human story, of poetry, learning, love, exile and suicide, his honest capacity to be moved. The incredible accomplishment of the *Works*, and also of the invaluable *Browning Box*, is complemented here by a dedication to his theme that is itself moving; and even as we rightly seek to transcend his critical idioms, contemporary readers of *Death's Jest-Book* must surely recognise Donner as a crucial foundation.

Certain critical interpretations of the *Jest-Book* have weathered noticeably well, others less so. Between two of the greats of modern Romantic criticism, Harold Bloom and Northrop Frye, it is Frye whose reading now seems to have survived best (and who is more positive about Beddoes's writing). In *The Visionary Company* (1962) Bloom reads Beddoes's poetry in terms of Romantic idealism, the drive to fuse subject and object, arguing that Beddoes eventually comes to identify death with the imagination; but his argument emphasises the failure of the poetry, based on a negative assessment of Beddoes's paralysis of theme, an assumption that Beddoes succumbed to despair and that his writing contains no hope of renewal. In *A Study of English Romanticism* (1968) Frye famously reads Beddoes's macabre theatre as an early prophetic stirring of the Absurd, and makes some fascinating use of Beddoes's grotesque comedy. His final assessment of Beddoes is unusually approving, and may be as close as *Death's Jest-Book* has ever come to the privilege of canonical status:

What Beddoes contributes to Romanticism is, perhaps, the most complete and searching poetic reaction to the Romantic sense of the limitations of ordinary experience. [...] It is Beddoes, as far as English literature is concerned, who brings us most directly into contact with the conception of the absurd in a way that permits of compassion but excludes self-pity.[12]

The well-established association of Beddoes's drama with
Modernist styles was lent renewed force recently, when the editors
of the Penguin selection of Hood, Praed and Beddoes chose to use
the 1890 Edmund Gosse edition as their copy text, arguing that it
significantly reflects the poet's relative prominence at the end of
the nineteenth century, 'its readers on the verge of the modernist
consciousness that would bring a fresh appreciation to Beddoes's
strange and compelling sensibility'.[13]

Beddoes's first commentators, the reviewers of *The Bride's
Tragedy*, were quick to identify a problem with his dramatic style:
although they were highly approving of the poetry, they also
remarked how Beddoes does not really succeed in differentiating
the 'voices' of his various characters. In bringing this charge, they
contributed to a debate about Romantic drama which still
continues today: are poets such as Coleridge, Wordsworth and
Shelley constitutionally unsuited to the writing of drama since, in
their unwillingness ever to relinquish intensity, they seem to give
all dramatic speech the qualities of 'overheard' soliloquy? An
intensity of image which produces this consistent impression of
an internalised action then raises further problems relating to the
location of an immaterial 'stage'. Several modern critics have
interpreted the difficult question of Beddoes's 'theatre' in mental
terms, arguing that the *Jest-Book* and other writings dramatise the
problematics of subjectivity. Eleanor Wilner (1975), who gives a
psychoanalytic/mythological reading, and Alan Richardson
(1988), who relates the drama to the legacy of Byron's 'mental
theatre', are two interesting examples from this field of enquiry.

Some understanding of both the scientific and occult principles
at work in *Death's Jest-Book* is clearly essential to any serious
reading. There is a complementary tension between these strands,
and both are integral to the drama's struggle with itself to
articulate a mythic meaning. Once again, these are interpretative
themes with early roots in Donner. Studies of Beddoes's 'Romantic
science' generally attempt either to draw lines of intellectual
descent from the researches of Thomas Beddoes Senior, or to focus
on documented sources of his medical studies in Germany and
Switzerland in an attempt to elucidate key principles in the text.
The theme will no doubt continue to exert a powerful hold on
readers (recent studies include those by Christopher Moylan, 1991;
and Michael Bradshaw, 2001). Similarly, the presence of occult
imagery and structures in *Death's Jest-Book* has long been

acknowledged, but has attracted some fresh analysis in recent years (such as that by Alan Halsey, 1996; and Moylan, 1998).

One area of enquiry which seems very likely to expand in the near future is that of gender and sexuality. The now prevalent sense of Beddoes's homosexuality was slow to emerge; a number of early commentators stop just short of the question of sex, hovering over the idea of Beddoes's habit of eroticising death, reluctant perhaps to go further. Beddoes's various 'close friendships' with men such as Card, Reich and Degen are – we may now feel – uncomfortably skirted round. And although the evidence is fairly circumstantial, many or most contemporary critics agree that Beddoes was probably gay. An article by Shelley Rees (2002) is a recent example of an idiom which seems certain to continue – the re-interpretation of *Death's Jest-Book* in terms of encoded homoerotic narratives, in this case drawing on the arguments of 'queer theory' that the presence of same-sex desire in a text can interrogate and subvert hitherto accepted norms of literary style and genre.

These are just a few of the more established methods of reading the text. We cannot know the future directions of interpretation, in the case of *Death's Jest-Book*, or anything else. It is to be hoped that Beddoes's drama will now keep step with contemporary critical practice and continue to be re-read through contemporary paradigms; but *The Fool's Tragedy* will surely retain its capacity to surprise. For the present, perhaps it is enough to note that international interest in the poet and his work has never been greater. Critical studies and conference papers have multiplied in recent years; in the summer of 2003 there were even stage performances (in Grasmere, Los Angeles and New York City) of a 'dramatic travesty' of the *Jest-Book*, written by Jerome J. McGann and directed by Frederick Burwick. This in turn can only stimulate further reading, re-reading and discussion. Although we should never underestimate the inertia of canon and reputation, the slow, belated assimilation of Beddoes into the mainstream of Romantic and nineteenth-century studies seems to have begun. *Death's Jest-Book*, the troubled centre of his achievement, may eventually come to assume a secure position among the 'major' texts of its era which are its near relatives in genre, theme and style, standards of the Romantic canon such as *The Cenci* and *Frankenstein*. We will see.

And so, the 'unhappy devil of a tragedy' lives again. But be warned – "'tis satirical'.[14]

Notes

1 The standard biographies by H.W. Donner (1935) and Royall H. Snow (1928) are listed below in the Select Bibliography. A new life of Beddoes is currently being written by John Baker. For an overview of critical responses to Beddoes, especially *DJ-B*, see 'Approaches to Beddoes' in my *Resurrection Songs* (2001), pp. 4–11; also a digest of criticism together with some preliminary remarks on 'minor' reputation in the Introduction to Beddoes, *Selected Poetry* (1999), pp. xvi–xxi.

2 Quotations from Beddoes in this introduction are all from Donner's *Works* (1935), listed below; page numbers will be cited in the text from now on.

3 But see Lytton Strachey (1907) and Ezra Pound (1913), two influential examples of the tendency to read the drama as 'ventriloquist' pastiche, discussed below and listed in the bibliography.

4 Works by Paracelsus were sold when Beddoes's books were auctioned to make good some of his debts after his departure from Göttingen in 1833; and he is known to have borrowed occult works by Cornelius Agrippa and others from the university library. See Jon W. Lundin, 'T.L. Beddoes at Göttingen' (1971), pp. 495–9; and works by Alan Halsey and Christopher Moylan (1998) listed in the bibliography.

5 Letter to Browning in Donner (ed.), *The Browning Box* (1935), pp. 108–9.

6 There was ample evidence of a continuing sense of blame in recent discussions of Procter on the Beddoes internet forum 'jestbook': http://groups.yahoo.com/group/jestbook/

7 For a summary of alternative ways of 'reading' the suppression of *DJ-B* in 1829, see my *Resurrection Songs* (2001), pp. 103–5. The story of what became of the drama after this crisis is taken up by a companion to the present volume, a new edition of the later text shortly to be published by West House: see Note on the Text below.

8 Donner outlines the evidence that 'MS II', his β text, was the copy sent to England for publication in his Introduction to *Works*, pp. xxxiii–iv.

9 'The Last Elizabethan'; all the critical works cited in this brief overview can be found in the bibliography.

10 *The Making of a Poet*, p. 201 and *passim*.

11 Ibid., p. 387.

12 Frye, pp. 84–5.

13 Wolfson and Manning, *Selected Poems of Hood, Praed and Beddoes* (1999), p. 254. *DJ-B* and Modernism: Beddoes makes a ghostly appearance in Pound's *Canto LXXX*, and also in Pound's cryptic annotation to the manuscript of Eliot's *The Waste Land*. See also essay by Christopher Ricks listed in the bibliography.

14 (Letter to Kelsall from Göttingen, October 1826, p. 620; Wolfram, V.iv.293.)

NOTE ON THE TEXT

Beddoes's autograph manuscripts have largely disappeared. All versions of *Death's Jest-Book* now derive either from the first published text, edited by Kelsall in 1850, or from a full transcription of Beddoes's papers made by James Dykes Campbell around 1886 – or from a combination of the two. The first editor to have had the benefit of Campbell's painstaking work with the manuscripts was H.W. Donner, and his *Works* (1935) remains the standard scholarly edition of Beddoes. In this monumental edition Donner identifies three distinct texts of the *Jest-Book*: two early versions of what is essentially the same five-act drama with incidental discrepancies, and one much larger later text, which represents an unfinished attempt to revise and expand on a grand scale. Donner names these texts α, β and γ respectively. The α text (1828) was the first fair copy. The β text (early 1829) was the original transcription for the press, the text Beddoes presumably envisaged as providing the copy for printed volumes. The γ text (1830–44) is the accumulation of later revisions.

The present edition of *Death's Jest-Book* follows the 1829 text, and has been prepared by a systematic separation of the β from the variorum *Jest-Book* in Donner's *Works*. My reasons for opting for this particular text are outlined briefly above. A new edition of Donner's γ text also appears in 2003, edited by Alan Halsey and published by West House: Alan and I corresponded during the preparation of these two editions, and we regard them as complementary. We hope that some readers might refer to both volumes, since, taken together they represent the full range of the *Jest-Book*'s changing disposition. Donner's *Works* combines the myriad variant readings into one massive *Jest-Book* with a parallel text of Act I. This is a variorum text, and not a conflation, and continues to be the ultimate resource for criticism of the drama. Yet I would argue that there is real value in separating the texts once again, to clarify and renew our sense of their contrasting styles. In his later edition of Beddoes's *Plays and Poems* for the Muses' Library (1950) Donner presented a quite different *Jest-Book*, and did in fact follow the 1829 text on the grounds that it was the version Beddoes had intended to see print; all later revisions were relegated to an appendix of fragments. The crucial difference between that edition and the present volume is that Donner omitted both Beddoes's Preface and his notes.

Beddoes's Preface, with its strident argument on the aesthetics of tragedy, should be considered an integral part of *Death's Jest-Book*. Dykes Campbell's transcription of 'Death's Jest-Book. MS. II', from which Donner derived his β text, opens with the Preface. Yet the Preface is strangely detached from its drama in *Works*, due to Donner's method of separating Beddoes's writings into generic groups ('Poems and Poetic Fragments', 'Dramas and Dramatic Fragments', 'Prose Works, Fragments and Letters'); and Donner chose to omit it entirely from *Plays and Poems*. I have reversed this, and reunited the Preface with *Death's Jest-Book*, as it was in 'MS. II'.

Beddoes provided several notes to his drama, which have been retained; all footnotes in the text are his own. Only the note on Bilderdijk in the Preface has been altered: here I have cut a very lengthy quotation in Dutch, but preserved the critical notes which follow (see *Works*, p. 532). The footnote about the *Baris* (II.i.54) is Beddoes's own, as is the end-note on the historical foundation of the plot, and the lengthy end-note on *Luz* and Jewish doctrines of resurrection. My own few editorial end-notes are signalled in the text with asterisks.

PUBLICATION HISTORY

1849   Shortly before his suicide in Basel, TLB bequeathed his manuscripts to Kelsall, to 'print or not as *he* thinks fit' (*Works*, p. 683).

1850   Kelsall's edition of *Death's Jest-Book; or, The Fool's Tragedy* (London: William Pickering), published anonymously: an invaluable but essentially corrupt text, in that Kelsall freely and openly suppressed or emended TLB's writing on aesthetic grounds.

1851   *The Poems Posthumous and Collected of Thomas Lovell Beddoes, with a Memoir*, ed. T.F. Kelsall, 2 vols (London: William Pickering): the second volume consisted of *The Brides' Tragedy*, bound with surplus copies of *DJ-B*. Kelsall's 'Memoir' was crucial, the foundation of all biographies of the poet.

1867   Procter introduced Kelsall to a fellow admirer of TLB, Robert Browning.

1873   Kelsall's widow sent the box of MSS and papers to Browning, Kelsall having hoped that Browning would edit them.

1881   Death of Zoë King, TLB's last surviving close relative; no further obstacle to a full publication of TLB, and a full revelation of the facts of his life and death.

1883   Browning invited Edmund Gosse to open the box of MSS with him; he later expressed the wish that Gosse would edit the complete works.

1886   James Dykes Campbell viewed the box after an enquiry to Browning, and began transcribing everything by or relating to TLB, supplementing and correcting Kelsall's edition of *DJ-B*, to produce the first variorum text.

1890   *The Poetical Works of Thomas Lovell Beddoes*, ed. with a memoir by Edmund Gosse, 2 vols (London: Dent): Gosse did not make use of Campbell's transcription, but essentially duplicated Kelsall's version of *DJ-B* with some minor alterations.

1907   *The Poems of Thomas Lovell Beddoes*, ed. with an introduction by Ramsay Colles (London: The Muses' Library, Routledge): significant in popularising TLB, but the texts are based on available printed versions, with no new work from MSS.

1912   Death of 'Pen' Browning, the poet's son, in Italy: the box of TLB's papers passed on to him by Gosse was found to have disappeared.

1928   *The Complete Works of Thomas Lovell Beddoes*, ed. with a memoir by Sir Edmund Gosse and decorated by the Dance of Death of Hans Holbein, 2 vols (London: Franfolico).

1935   *The Works of Thomas Lovell Beddoes*, ed. with an introduction by H.W. Donner (London: Oxford University Press): the definitive edition, making full use of Dykes Campbell's transcriptions, and presenting *DJ-B* as a three-text variorum; published simultaneously with Donner's biography of TLB, and *The Browning Box*, a collection of letters devoted to TLB's legacy and the transmission of the texts (see Select Bibliography).

1950   *Plays and Poems of Thomas Lovell Beddoes*, ed. with an introduction by H.W. Donner (London: 'The Muses' Library', Routledge and Kegan Paul): a reader's edition, without the scholarly apparatus of *Works*; presents only the 1829 *DJ-B*, with an appendix of later fragments; a valuable alternative to the variorum in *Works*.

1978   Reprint of Donner's *Works* (New York: AMS Press): the last complete publication of the drama; since then *DJ-B* has been published in extract form only.

SELECT BIBLIOGRAPHY

Agar, John, 'Isbrand and T.L. Beddoes' Aspiring Hero', *Studia Neophilologica*, 45 (1973), 370–82

Beddoes, Thomas Lovell, *Selected Poetry*, revd edn, ed. Judith Higgens and Michael Bradshaw (Manchester: Carcanet, 1999)

—— *The Works of Thomas Lovell Beddoes*, ed. with an introduction by H.W. Donner (London: Oxford University Press, 1935; repr. New York: AMS Press, 1978)

Bloom, Harold, *The Visionary Company: A Reading of English Romantic Poetry* (London and New York: Faber and Faber, 1962)

Bradshaw, Michael, *Resurrection Songs: The Poetry of Thomas Lovell Beddoes* (Aldershot: Ashgate, 2001)

Bush, Douglas, 'Minor Poets of the Early Nineteenth Century', in *Mythology and the Romantic Tradition in English Poetry* (New York: Pageant, 1957), pp. 169–96

Coxe, Louis O., 'Beddoes: The Mask of Parody', *The Hudson Review*, 6 (1953), 251–66

Donner, H.W. (ed. with an introduction), *The Browning Box; or, The Life and Works of Thomas Lovell Beddoes as reflected in letters by his friends and admirers* (London: Oxford University Press, 1935)

—— *Thomas Lovell Beddoes: The Making of a Poet* (Oxford: Basil Blackwell, 1935; repr. Folcroft, 1970)

Forster, John, 'The Literary Examiner: *Death's Jest-Book, or The Fool's Tragedy*', *The Examiner*, 20 July 1850, 461–63

Frye, Northrop, 'Yorick: The Romantic Macabre', in *A Study of English Romanticism* (New York: Random House, 1968; repr. London: Harvester, 1983), pp. 51–85

Gregory, Horace, 'The Gothic Imagination and the Survival of Thomas Lovell Beddoes' in *The Dying Gladiators, and Other Essays* (New York: Grove, 1961), pp. 81–95

Halsey, Alan, *Homage to Homunculus Mandrake* (Belper: Thomas Lovell Beddoes Society, 1996)

Harrex, Anne, '*Death's Jest-Book* and the German Contribution', *Studia Neophilologica*, 39 (1967), 15–37 and 302–18

Heath-Stubbs, John, 'The Defeat of Romanticism', in *The Darkling Plain: A Study of the Later Fortunes of Romanticism in English Poetry from George Darley to W.B. Yeats* (London: Eyre and Spottiswoode, 1950), pp. 21–61

Jack, Ian, 'Clare and the Minor Poets', in *English Literature 1815–32: Scott, Byron and Keats* (London: Oxford University Press, The Oxford History of English Literature, 1963), pp. 130–84

Lundin, Jon W., 'T.L. Beddoes at Göttingen', *Studia Neophilologica*, 43 (1971), 484–99

Moylan, Christopher, 'T.L. Beddoes, Romantic Medicine, and the Advent of Therapeutic Theater', *Studia Neophilologica*, 69 (1991), 181–8

—— *Thomas Lovell Beddoes and the Hermetic Tradition* (*Seeds, Bones, Bowls: T.L. Beddoes' Alchemical Recipe*) (Belper: Thomas Lovell Beddoes Society, 1998)

—— '"For Luz is a Good Joke": Thomas Lovell Beddoes and Jewish Eschatology', in *British Romanticism and the Jews*, ed. Sheila Spector (New York: Palgrave, 2002), pp. 93–103

O'Neill, Michael, '"A Storm of Ghosts": Beddoes, Shelley, Death, and Reputation', *The Cambridge Quarterly*, 28, 2 (1999), 102–15

Potter, G.R., 'Did Thomas Lovell Beddoes Believe in the Evolution of the Species?', *Modern Philology*, 21 (1923), 89–100

Pound, Ezra, 'Beddoes and Chronology' (1913), in *Selected Prose*, ed. William Cookson (London: Faber and Faber, 1973), pp. 348–53

Rees, Shelley, 'Melveric and Wolfram: A Love Story', *The Thomas Lovell Beddoes Society*, 8 (2002), 14–25

Richardson, Alan, '*Death's Jest-Book*: "Shadows of Words"', in *A Mental Theater: Poetic Drama and Consciousness in the Romantic Age* (University Park, Penn. and London: Pennsylvania State University Press, 1988), pp. 154–73

Ricks, Christopher, 'Thomas Lovell Beddoes: "A dying start"', *Grand Street*, 1 (1982), 32–48; and 3 (1984), 90–102; repr. in *The Force of Poetry* (Oxford: Oxford University Press, 1984), pp. 135–62

Snow, Royall H., *Thomas Lovell Beddoes, Eccentric and Poet* (New York: Covici-Friede, 1928)

Strachey, Lytton, 'The Last Elizabethan' (1907), in *Books and Characters, French and English* (London: Chatto and Windus, 1922), pp. 225–52

Thompson, James R., *Thomas Lovell Beddoes* (Boston: Twayne, 1985)

Wagner, Geoffrey, 'Centennial of A Suicide: Thomas Lovell Beddoes', *Horizon*, 19 (1949), 417–35

Wilner, Eleanor, *Gathering the Winds: Visionary Imagination and Radical Transformation of Self and Society* (Baltimore and London: The Johns Hopkins University Press, 1975)

Wolfson, Susan J. and Manning, Peter J. (eds), *Selected Poems of Hood, Praed and Beddoes* (Harmondsworth: Penguin, 1999)

DEATH'S JEST-BOOK

*Preface**

Apprehending that the style and form of the following drama, somewhat unusual amongst us in later days, may appear not a little distasteful and objectionable to some of those few readers whom an unknown writer is likely to meet with, I shall venture to recapitulate a few literary principles which a certain set of critics, once and probably still of considerable influence, have either out of ignorance overlooked, or wilfully and unpardonably suppressed. Too many of these men indeed have been utterly unfitted for their calling by the perverse direction of their learning: an early, long and exclusive study of Greek and Roman works prejudiced them in favour of the literature of the South; their knowledge of modern foreign literature has been confined to that of the French, Italian &c, and they have in consequence, selected for their standard such among the numerous writers in our language as leaned to the taste of one or other of these peoples whose origin, bodily and intellectual disposition, climate, religion, and destiny in the history of the world, so widely differ from our own. This estrangement from the monuments of our own national genius and those of the other nations related to us by blood and language could not but occasion the most extravagant errors of judgement among our most popular literary dictators, and thus the Poetics of Aristotle were regarded constantly as our dramatic code while Shakspeare occupied the stage, and we were pusillanimous enough to sanction apologies for his alleged heresies, instead of proclaiming him at once the best model and only legitimate authority for English playwriters. Supposed inexhaustible learning was the cabbalistic watchword which disarmed the few who would have offered opposition, and made 'such cowards of us all'. Men who would have laughed to scorn any pedantic attempt to remodel their national constitution according to the political fancies of Plato, confessed in all humility to the critical creed of his disciple. But the spirit of a people is immortal and unconquerable, it modifies itself to no laws of man, for it is itself after some moral law of Nature, produced by a certain combination of events as necessarily as the phœnomena of

Galvanism or electricity are consequent on a particular natural or artificial arrangement of the materials which elicit or convey them.

These remarks are more especially applicable to the fate of the drama in our country: the writer of them knows well and values highly the advantage resulting from a *comparative* study of ancient and modern foreign writers. He is ready to admit that the Epic and many varieties of Lyric poetry are subject to extraneous laws, for such is their extraction, but it is very easy to prove that the ballad and its varieties, and the play in its national form (i.e. that of Shakspeare) are aboriginal productions of the modern nations; and moreover, that the latter has not only a different origin from the drama of the Greeks, but even one diametrically opposite to that. They were both religious festivities, the Grecian consisting in its rudest state of the simple hymn to Bacchus, and in the modern the pantomimical exhibition of some event in Sacred history. Such was the nucleus of each genus of dramatic composition, and the difference in the form of each depended upon this. The Grecian theatre had an altar for its centre — round this was chaunted the hymn to Bacchus or another Deity, interrupted and exemplified by the solemn representation of some legend of the gods or demi-gods. The stature of the actors, their features, their voices and the feelings they had to express, were other than human. On the other hand, the dumb show of the lay brothers at Easter and other Church feasts gradually adopted words, but these were used only to express the passions, or explain the situations in which the persons were to appear involved: further than this no aid was sought from the art of eloquence: and the stage thus founded has ever retained the features of its infancy: 'tis active, impatient of any but impassioned poetry, full of pomp and show, and appealing wherever it is possible, to the evidence of the external senses. In short to use the words of Bilderdijk[1] to whose learning and

---

[1] [...]* The whole of this essay is eminently worthy of attention, as indeed are almost all of the numerous works of this extraordinary poet of Holland; excepting I am afraid the tragedies which precede this very excellent critical and historical disquisition. The English reader will, however, hardly be of the same opinion with him in regard to the merits of Shakspeare and Schiller, and the poetry of the two nations which these two great men may be fairly considered to represent. Pity indeed, that a man so singularly learned and able should be so bigoted and sectarian in literature.

Besides Bilderdijk, and A.W. Schlegel, many observations of the highest value on these points may be found scattered in various writings of Tieck, whose promised work on Shakspeare every admirer of that poet must most earnestly desire.

acuteness we are indebted for the elucidation of this important historical fact, 'The tragedy of the Greeks was a Lyrical Poem — it represents a single and simple action, developing it regularly; and represents this action in the manner peculiar to such poetry, and so in subordination to the requisites of this kind of poetry, that the poetry is not made for the sake of the action, but the action for the sake of the poem, while, on the other hand, the historical play is an event represented to the eye and ear. The composition is made entirely for the sake of the action, not the action for the sake of the composition.' The former is a goat song, the latter a stage play.

Our English play then, is the work of art emanating from materials so simple, but as a work of art, not destitute of its general rules, resulting all from the nature of its first foundation, and therefore, to the confusion of all critics of the Aristotelian or Horatian school, utterly and precisely the reverse of those to which the Tragedy of the Ancients was amenable. It is not Shakspeare who is lawless, they are lawless who judge his British example by the precept of the Greeks, and summon him who should be their law-giver, before their bar who are literary outlaws.

It may not be out of place here to suggest, that, as the modern play has for its theme, man and his interests, and exhibits him exposed solely to the operation of those great moral laws so easy to be traced in the history of the world, which render him individually or socially subject to the consequences of his own actions (and here, where the soul is constantly at work under our eyes, we cannot as in actual life, be deceived by the external appearance of misery or happiness:) it follows that the principle of fatality, so warmly recommended once by A.W. v. Schlegel and so unsuccessfully wrought on by Müllner, Werner, Grillparzer and other German dramatists in their 'plays of destiny' (*Schicksal-Stücken*) is utterly irreconcilable with a leading idea of the romantic Drama.

Another source of illustrating the poetry, happily adopted by a German critic just mentioned,* is to be found in the national mode of cultivating the other arts. They are in like manner under the influence of the religion and climate of a Country. Now, our genuine style in Architecture and sculpture is undoubtedly the Gothic, and who can deny the analogy between an old English Play and one of our ancient Cathedrals? Intricate, vast and gloomy, both intimate the supernatural and are full of indistinct thoughts of immortality; both present in the general view, large masses which inspire sentiments of awe and a sense of overpowering sublimity: and yet each of these grand divisions has its minor component parts; each elaborately ornamented with the counterfeit of some agreeable image in nature, or figures that owe their being alone to a wild fancy, sometimes light and joyous, sometimes fearfully hideous — often satirical, grotesque or ludicrous. The choice and method of combining these materials so essential to each art, are again, alike characteristic: they arise from that disposition to interpret the phœnomena of nature as types in reference to humanity which is so strikingly expressed in modern poetry and philosophy.

Nothing is to be so assiduously avoided in the cultivation of taste than a sectarian narrow-heartedness, which can be fairly attributed to those only who persist in deterioration or eulogy of any literature or single production without reference to and out of connection with the people and the period in which it originated. Free from all dread of such an imputation, then be it here fearlessly pronounced once for all, that the Shakspearian form of the Drama, under such unimportant modifications as the circumstances of our times demand, is the best, nay, the only English one: and arduous as the task may be, the observation of his example is the only course which can ever insure to the dramatist any real popularity among his countrymen. To many this assertion will appear neither novel nor necessary — that it is the latter, at least, the remarkable facts resulting from an examination of our dramatic library will prove: that, with scarce one exception, but that of a living writer who will occur to the reader,* the generations of dramatists that have existed since the times of James the first have assimilated the forms of their pieces to the French, the Greek, the Spanish &ᶜ, but never thought of recurring to the old and only canon.

These remarks it is to be hoped the favourable reader will apply with the greatest modification to the judgement of the poem before him. This is undoubtedly a very faulty one, nor is it intended to be otherwise; it is offered as a specimen of what might be called the florid Gothic in poetry, which the author desires to leave alone and hopes therefore, probably quite superfluously, that it will meet with no imitators. It is written for those who can find entertainment in it — and in the humble hope that the greater number of critics (or, to speak more properly) reviewers will be kind enough to find it guilty of almost every literary offence according to their critical judgement; and thus assure the otherwise inconsolable author that he has succeeded in producing something which has at least the merit of being at variance with their taste. Only one thing he begs of these gentlemen, to spare him the vexation of being eulogized by them, and to avoid any such misfortune engages to deliver gratuitously to the dealers in reviews an article on and by himself replete with the choicest flowers of obloquy, depreciation of the style, hints of plagiarism, and especially (as the forlorn hope) appeals to the classical taste of the polished world, who have learned the Odes of Horace by heart at Eton &^{c}, differing therefore materially from the tone in which certain writers in a great Review are in the habit of holding inquest on their own works. The reader will therefore recognise directly the hand which produces the most violent attack, and with this warning hint the writer bids him farewell, and defiance to such of his reviewers as shall venture to praise him.

Death's Jest-Book
or
The Fool's Tragedy
In Five Acts

―― Δημαγωγεῖ
ἐν τοῖς ἄνω. νεκροῖσι,   420
κἀστὶν τὰ πρῶτα τῆς ἐκεῖ μοχθηρίας.

＊　　＊　　＊

Χωρῶμεν ἐς πολυρρόδους
λειμῶνας ἀνθεμώδεις,   450
τὸν ἡμέτερον τρόπον,
τὸν καλλιχορώτατον,
παίζοντες, ὃν ὄλβιαι
Μοῖραι ξυνάγουσιν.
ΜΟΝΟΙΣ ΓΑΡ ῾ΗΜΙΝ ῾ΗΛΙΟΣ
ΚΑΙ ΦΕΓΓΟΣ ῾ΙΛΑΡΟΝ ᾽ΕΣΤΙΝ
῾ΟΣΟΙ ΜΕΜΥΗΜΕΘ᾽.

Χορος Μυστων.

Aristoph. Ranae. Ed. Dindorf Lips. 1824-8.

PERSONS REPRESENTED

MELVERIC, *Duke of Münsterberg*
ADALMAR ⎫ *His sons*
ATHULF ⎭
WOLFRAM, *a knight* ⎫ *Brothers*
ISBRAND, *the court-fool* ⎭
TORWALD, *Governor in the Duke's absence*
MARIO
SIEGFRIED
ZIBA
HOMUNCULUS MANDRAKE, *zany to a mountebank*
[BOY]

SIBYLLA

AMALA, *Torwald's daughter*
KATE

Knights, Arabs, Attendants, Musicians, Priests, Sailors, Conspirators, Grave-diggers, Pall-bearers, Guards, Messengers, Ladies, attending on Sibylla and on Amala

The Dance of Death

SCENE: *in the first act at Ancona, and afterwards in Egypt; in the latter acts at the town of Grüssau, residence of the Duke of Münsterberg, in Silesia.*

TIME: *the end of the thirteenth century.*

ACT I

SCENE I. *The Seashore. Ancona*

Enter MANDRAKE *and* KATE

MANDRAKE Am I a man of gingerbread that you should mould me to your liking, or hath my will a man's nose to follow? To have my way, in spite of your tongue and reason's teeth, tastes better than Hungary wine; and my heart beats in a honey-pot now I reject you and all sober 5 sense: so, I prithee, go back to my master, the Doctor, and tell him he may seek another zany for his booth, a new wise merry Andrew. My jests are cracked, my coxcomb fallen, my bauble confiscated, my cap mediatized. Toll the bell; for Jack Pudding is no more! 10

KATE Wilt thou away from *me* then, sweet Mandrake? Wilt thou not marry me?

MANDRAKE Child, my studies must first be ended. Thou knowest I hunger after wisdom, as the red sea after ghosts; therefore will I travel awhile. 15

KATE Whither then, dear Mandrake?

MANDRAKE Whither should a student in the black arts, an adept, a Rosicrucian? Where is our native land? You heard the herald this morning thrice invite all christian folk to follow the brave knight, Sir Wolfram, to the shores of Egypt, 20 and there help to free from bondage his noble fellow in arms, Duke Melveric, whom, on a pilgrimage to the Holy Sepulchre, wild pagans captured. There, Kate, in that Sphynx land they made the roads with the philosopher's stone. There be wise crocodiles whose daughters are more 25 cunning than the witches of Lapland, and fairer than the Lotus of the Nile. There can one chat with mummies in a pyramid, and breakfast on basilisk's eggs. Thither then, Homunculus Mandrake, son of the great Paracelsus; languish no more in the ignorance of these climes, but 30 abroad with alembic and crucible, and weigh anchor for Egypt.

Enter ISBRAND

ISBRAND Good morrow, brother Vanity! How? soul of a pickle-herring, body of a spagirical toss-pot, doublet of motley, and mantle of pilgrim, how art thou transmuted! 35

Wilt thou desert our brotherhood, fool sublimate? Shall the
motley chapter no longer boast thee? Wilt thou forswear the
order of the bell, and break thy vows to Momus? Have mercy
on Wisdom and relent.

MANDRAKE Have reverence, I pray thee. To-morrow I   40
know thee not. In truth, I mark our noble faculty is in decay.
The world will see its ears in a glass no longer; so we are laid
aside and shall soon be forgotten; for why should the feast
of asses come but once a year, when all the days are foaled
of one mother? O world, world! The gods and fairies left   45
thee, for thou wert too wise; and now, thou Socratic star, thy
demon, the great Pan, Folly, is parting from thee. The oracles
still talked in their sleep, shall our grandchildren say, till
Master Merriman's kingdom was broken up: now is every
man his own fool, and the world's cheerless.   50

ISBRAND Farewell, thou great-eared mind: I mark, by thy
talk, that thou commencest philosopher, and then thou art
only a fellow-servant out of livery. But lo! here come the
uninitiated — now avaunt, wise spirit, thou hast no portion
in me.   55

Enter TORWALD, AMALA, WOLFRAM, *Knights and Ladies*

TORWALD The turning tide; the sea's wide leafless wind,
Wherein no birds inhabit and few traffic,
Making his cave within your sunny sails;
The eager waves, whose golden, silent kisses
Seal an alliance with your bubbling oars;   60
And our still-working wishes, that impress
Their meaning on the conscience of the world,
And prompt the unready Future, — all invite you
Unto your voyage. And prosperous be the issue,
As is the promise, and the purpose good!   65
Are all the rest aboard?

WOLFRAM   All. 'Tis a train
Of knights whose bosoms pant with one desire,
Bold hearts and ardent all; their high resolve
So rocky and embattled in the flood
Of their desire: a flaming ghost-walked sea: 70
That Fate's decrees against us, shod in iron
With sails of dragon's wings, and manned with devils,
Would scarce escape a wreck. All hearts are ready.

MANDRAKE All, sir Knight; but the pigs are just going

aboard, and poor dear great Mandrake must be shipped too. 75
 WOLFRAM Who is this fellow that interrupts?
 ISBRAND One of the many you have made. Yesterday he
was a fellow of my kindred and served a quacksalver, but
now he lusts after the mummy land whither you are bound.
'Tis a servant of the rosy cross, a correspondent with the 80
stars; the dead are his friends, and the secrets of the moon
his knowledge. He will brew you a gallon of gold out of a
shilling. But had I been cook to a chameleon, I could not
sweeten the air to his praise enough. Suffice it, of his wisdom
Solomon knew less than a bee of petrified flowers, or your 85
butcher of the Mammoth. We fools send him as ambassador
to Africa; take him with you, or be yourself our
representative.
 WOLFRAM Speedily aboard then; and sink us not with thy
understanding. 90
 MANDRAKE I thank thee, Knight. Twice shalt thou live for
this, if I bottle eternity.   [*Exit with* KATE.
 TORWALD These letters, then, are the last trust I give you:
Of his two sons, whose love and dread ambition,
Crossing like murderous swords, teach us affright; 95
And of the uncertain people, who incline
Daily more to the present influence,
Forgetting all that their sense apprehends not;
I have at large discoursed unto the Duke:
And may you find his spirit strong to bear 100
The roughness of such tidings.
 ISBRAND (*aside*) May they flatten him till he have no more
brain than a pancake.
 AMALA   And forget not
Our duke, with gentle greetings, to remind 105
Of those who have no sword to draw for him,
But whose unarmed love is not less true,
Than theirs who seek him helmed. And so farewell,
They say you serve a lady in those lands,
So we dare offer you no token, knight, 110
Beside good wishes.
 WOLFRAM   Thanks, and farewell to both;
And so I take my leave.
     [*Exeunt* AMALA, TORWALD *and Attendants.*
 ISBRAND Stay: you have not my blessing yet. With what

jest shall I curse you in earnest? Know you this garb, and him
who wears it, and wherefore it is worn? A father slain and   115
plundered; our fraternal bond against the assassin shall so
end that thou savest him whom we should help to damn? O
do it, and I shall learn to laugh the dead out of their coffins!

WOLFRAM Hence with your idle taunts. I must away.
The wind so fair, the sun so bright, the waves   120
Caress invitingly into their bosom
My fleet ship's keel, that at her anchor bounds
As doth the greyhound from his leader's hand,
Following his eye beams after the light roe.

ISBRAND Away then, away! Thus be our fair purpose   125
shipwrecked. Unfurl your sails and let all the honest finny
folk of ocean, and those fair witty fishes, the mermaid
spinsters, follow your luckless boats with mockery: there's
not a blubber but shall wish he had a voice to yell parricide
in your sails, not a sea-dog but shall howl and hunt you   130
down after his salt-water fashion when he knows your
errand. What, O! what spirit of our ancestral enemies would
dare to whisper this tale through our father's bones? Thou
wilt save him from the Saracens' chains, who robbed our
sire's grey hairs of a crown, and trod him down a beggar to   135
the sceptred corpses of our progenitors? Save *him*, who slew
our hopes; bless him who cozened us of our part of this
sepulchral planet? Revenge, Revenge! lend me your torch,
that I may by its bloody light spell the lines of this man's face,
and note how pitiful an ass the philtres of charity and   140
friendship have made of my poor brother.

WOLFRAM Should we repent this change? I know not why.—
We came disguised into the court, stiff limbed
With desperate intent, and doubly souled
With murder's devil and our own still ghosts.   145
But must I not relent, finding the heart,
For which my dagger hungered, so inclined
In brotherly affection unto me?
O bless the womanish weakness of my soul,
Which came to slay, and leads me now to save!   150

ISBRAND Hate! Hate! Revenge and blood! These are the
only words of any language I will teach my boys. What
accursed poison has that Duke, that snake, with his tongue,
his sting, dropped into thine ear? Thou art no brother of mine

more: he was a fellow whose soul was of that tune which   155
shall awake the dead; aye if you had played it on a sow-
gelder's horn: for thine! if I should make a trumpet of the
devil's antlers, and blow thee through it, my lady's poodle
would be scarce moved to a hornpipe. O fie on't! Say when
hast thou undergone transfusion, and whose hostile blood   160
now turns thy life's wheels? Who has poured Lethe into thy
veins to wash thy father out of heart and brains? Ha! be pale,
and smile, and be prodigal of thy body's motions, for thou
hast no soul more. *That* thy sire placed in thee; and, with the
determination to avenge, thou hast turned it out of doors.   165
But 'tis well: why lament? Now I have all the hatred and
revenge of the world to myself to hate and murder him with.

    WOLFRAM Thou speak'st unjustly, what thou rashly think'st;
But time must soften and convince: now leave me,
If thou hast nothing but reproach for pastime.   170

    ISBRAND Be angry then, and we will curse each other. But
if thou goest now to save this man, come not again for fear
of me and the paternal ghost: for when he comes to me in the
night, and cries revenge! my heart forgets that my head hath
a fool's cap on it, and dreams of daggers: come not again   175
then!

    WOLFRAM Out of my path! In this despised garb
Alone, durst thou have tempted thus my anger,
Dishonour'd brother! While I am away,
Meditate o'er thy servile state, thou groom,   180
Crown'd and anointed priest of mockery:
And mend thee if thou canst. — I am for Egypt.   [*Exit.*

    ISBRAND Contempt then be thy shadow in the day
And point at thee and call thee parricide!
But I will turn my bosom now to thee,   185
Brutus, thou saint of the avenger's order;
Refresh me with thy spirit, or pour in
Thy whole great ghost. Isbrand, thou tragic fool,
Cheer up! Art thou alone? Why, so should be
Creators and destroyers. I'll go brood   190
And strain my burning and distracted soul
Against the naked spirit of the world,
Till some portent's begotten.   [*Exit.*

SCENE II. *The African Coast: a woody solitude near the sea. In the back ground ruins overshadowed by the characteristic vegetation of the oriental regions*

   The DUKE *and* SIBYLLA; *the latter sleeping in a tent*
 DUKE Soft sleep enwrap thee: with his balm bedew
Thy young fair limbs, Sibylla: thou didst need
The downy folding of his arms about thee.
And wake not yet, for still the starless night
Of our misfortune holds its hopeless noon.   5
No serpent shall creep o'er the sand to sting thee,
No blossom-trampling lion, no sea-creature,
(For such are now the partners of thy chamber,)
Disturb thy rest: only the birds shall dare
To shake the dewy blossoms that hang o'er thee,   10
And fan thee with their wings. As I watch for thee,
So may the power, that has so far preserved us,
Now in the uttermost, now that I feel
The cold drops on my forehead, and scarce know
Whether Fear shed them there, or the near breath 15
Of our pursuing foes has settled on it,
Stretch its shield o'er us.
      Enter ZIBA
      What bring'st, Ziba? Hope?
Else be as dumb as that thou bring'st, Despair.
 ZIBA Fruits: as I sat among the boughs, and robbed
The sparrows and their brothers of their bread,   20
A horde of armed Saracens rode by,
Each swearing that thy sword should rest ere night
Within his sheath, his weapon in thy breast.
 DUKE Speak lower, Ziba, lest the lady wake.
Perhaps she sleeps not, but with half-shut eyes   25
Will hear her fate. The slaves shall need to wash
My sword of Moslem blood before they sheath it.
Which path took they?
 ZIBA   Sleeping, or feigning sleep,
She doth well: 'tis trying on a garb
Which she must wear, sooner or later, long: 30
'Tis but a warmer lighter death.
        The ruffians,
Of whom I spoke, turned towards the cedar forest,

And, as they went in, there rushed forth a lion
And tore their captain down. Long live the lion!
We'll drink his tawny health: he gave us wine.   35
For, while the Moors in their black fear were flying,
I crept up to the fallen wretch, and borrowed
His flask of rubious liquor. May the prophet
Forgive him, as I do, for carrying it!
This for to-day: to-morrow hath gods too,   40
Who'll ripen us fresh berries, and uncage
Another lion on another foe.
    DUKE Brave Arab, thanks. But saw'st thou from the heights
No christian galley steering for this coast?
    ZIBA I looked abroad upon the wide old world,   45
And in the sky and sea, through the same clouds,
The same stars saw I glistening, and nought else.
And as my soul sighed unto the world's soul,
Far in the north a wind blackened the waters,
And after that creating breath was still,   50
A dark speck sat on the sky's edge: as watching
Upon the heaven-girt border of my mind
The first faint thought of a great deed arise,
With force and fascination I drew on
The wished sight, and my hope seemed to stamp   55
Its shape upon it. Not yet is it clear
What, or from whom, the vessel.
    DUKE   Who so e'er
The ocean wanderers, Heaven give them welcome:
There's nothing we can fear. Who dare refuse us
Protection from the savage Moslem's rage?   60
But see, the lady stirs. Once more look out,
And thy next news be safety.   [*Exit* ZIBA.
                      Hast thou gathered
Rest and refreshment from thy desart couch,
My fair Sibylla?
    SIBYLLA   Deeply have I slept.
As one who doth go down unto the springs   65
Of his existence and there bathed, I come
Regenerate up into the world again.
Kindest protector, 'tis to thee I owe
This boon, a greater than my parents gave.
Me, who had never seen this earth, this heaven,   70

The sun, the stars, the flowers, but shut from nature
Within my dungeon birthplace lived in darkness,
Me hast thou freed from the oppressor's power,
And godlike given me this heaven, this earth,
The flowers, the stars, the sun. Methinks it were   75
Ingratitude to thank thee for a gift
So measurelessly great.
    DUKE   As yet, sweet lady,
I have deserved but little thanks of thine.
We've not yet broken prison. This wall of waves
Still lies between us and the world of men;   80
That too I hope to climb. Our true Egyptian
Hath brought me news of an approaching ship.
When that hath borne thee to our German shore,
And thou amongst the living tastest life,
And gallants shall have shed around thy beauties   85
A glory of the starry looks of love,
For thee to move in, thank me then.
    SIBYLLA   I wish not
To leave this shady quiet way of life.
Why should we seek cruel mankind again?
Nature is kinder far: and every thing   90
That lives around us, with its pious silence,
Gives me delight: the insects, and the birds
That come unto our table, seeking food,
The flowers, upon whose petals Night tells down
Her tremulous dews, these are my dearest playmates.   95
O let us never leave them.
    DUKE   That would be
To rob thy fate of thee. In other countries
Another godliker mankind doth dwell,
Whose works each day adorn and deify
The world their fathers left them. Thither shalt thou,   100
For among them must be the one thou'rt born for.
Durst thou be such a traitress to thy beauty
As to live here unloving and unloved?
    SIBYLLA Love I not thee? O, if I feel beside thee
Delight and an unruffled calm, in which   105
My soul doth gather round thee, to reflect
Thy heavenly goodness: if in thy society
I am so full of comfort, that no room

For any other wish, no doubt, remains;
Love I not thee?
    DUKE   Dear maiden, thou art young.   110
Thou must see many, and compare their merits
Ere thou canst choose. Esteem and quiet friendship
Oft bear Love's semblance for awhile.
    SIBYLLA   I know it;
Thou shalt hear how. A year and more is past
Since a brave Saxon knight did share my prison;   115
A noble generous man, in whose discourse
I found much pleasure: yet, when he was near me,
There ever was a pain which I perceived
Even in the very sweetness of my comfort:
My heart was never still: and many times,   120
When he had fetched me flowers, I trembled so
That oft they fell as I was taking them
Out of his hand. When I would speak to him
I heard not, and I knew not what I said.
Yet this I thought was Love. O self deceived!   125
For now I can speak all I think to thee
With confidence and ease. What else can that be
Except true love?
    DUKE   The like I bear to thee,
O more than all that thou hast promised me:
For if another being stepped between us,   130
And were he my best friend, I must forget
All vows, and cut his heart away from mine.
    SIBYLLA Think not on that: it is impossible.
                  Enter ZIBA
    ZIBA O my dear lord, we're saved!
    DUKE   How? Speak!
Though every word hath now no meaning more,   135
Since thou hast said 'she's saved'.
    ZIBA The ship is in the bay, an armed knight
Steps from his boat upon the shore.
    DUKE   Blest hour!
And yet how palely, with what faded lips
Do we salute this unhoped change of fortune!   140
Thou art so silent, lady; and I utter
Shadows of words, like to an ancient ghost,
Arisen out of hoary centuries

Where none can speak his language. I had thought
That I should laugh, and shout, and leap on high: 145
But see! this breath of joy hath damped my soul,
Melted the icy mail, with which despair
Had propped my heart, unsealed the springs of weakness:
And O! how weary, sad and faint I go
To welcome what I prayed for. Thou art quiet;   150
How art thou then, my love?
    SIBYLLA   Now Hope and Fear
Stand by me, masked in one another's shapes;
I know not which is which, and, if I did,
I doubt which I should choose.
          Enter WOLFRAM *and Knights with* ZIBA
    WOLFRAM   Are these thy comrades?
Then, Arab, thy life's work and mine is done.   155
My duke, my fellow knight!
    DUKE   O friend! So call me!
Wolfram, thou comest to us like a god,
Giving life where thou touchest with thy hand.
    WOLFRAM Were it mine own, I'd break it here in twain,
And give you each a half.
    DUKE   I will not thank thee,   160
I will not welcome thee, embrace and bless thee;
Nor will I weep in silence. Gratitude,
Friendship, and Joy are beggar'd, and turned forth
Out of my heart for silly hypocrites:
They understand me not; and my soul, dazzled,   165
Stares on the unknown feelings that now crowd it,
Knows none of them, remembers none, counts none,
More than a new-born child in its first hour.
One word, and then we'll speak of this no more:
At parting each of us did tear a leaf   170
Out of a magic roll, and, robbing life
Of the red juice with which she feeds our limbs,
We wrote a mutual bond. Thou dost remember?
    WOLFRAM And if a promise binds beyond the grave
My ghost shall not forget it. There I swore   175
That, if I died before thee, I would come
With the first weed that shoots out of my grave,
And bring thee tidings of our other home.
    DUKE That bond hast thou now fulfilled thus; or rather

Unto me lying in my sepulchre   180
Comest thou, and say'st, 'Arise and live again'.
    WOLFRAM And with thee dost thou bring some angel back.
Look on me, lady.
    SIBYLLA (*aside*) Pray heaven, she be not
The angel of the death of one of you,
To make the grave and the flowers' roots amends. —   185
Now turn I to thee, knight. O dared I hope,
Thou hast forgotten me!
    WOLFRAM   Then were I dead,
And stripped of the human spirit's inheritance,
The immortality, of which thy love
Gave me the first sure proof. Forgotten thee!   190
Aye; if thou be not she, with whom I shared
Few months ago that dungeon, which thy presence
Lit with delight unknown to liberty;
If thou be not Sibylla, she whose semblance
Here keepeth watch upon my heart. Behold it: 195
Morning and night my eyes do feed upon it.
Thou gavest it me one day, when I admired,
And coveted above all stars a dewdrop,
That in the joyous dimple of a flower
Imaged thee tremulously. Since that time   200
Many a secret tear hath done the same,
Which I have shed over this pictured beauty. —
Speak to me then: or art thou, as this toy,
Only the likeness of the maid I loved?
But there's no seeming such a one. O come!   205
This talking is a pitiful invention:
We'll leave it to the wretched. All my science,
My memory, I'd give for thy sole love,
And keep that ever secret.
    SIBYLLA   Thou dost move me.
With ghost-compelling words thou draw'st me to thee: 210
O! at thy call I must surrender me,
My lord, my love, my life.
    DUKE (*aside*)   O souls that dwell
In these three bosoms, keep your footings fast,
For there's a blasting thought stirring among you.
They love each other. Silence! Let them love;   215
And let him be her love. She is a flower,

Growing upon a grave. — Now, gentle lady,
Retire, beseech you, to the tent and rest.
My friend and I have need to use those words
Which are bequeathed unto the miserable.   220
Come hither; you have made me free of them:
Who dare be wretched in the world beside me?
Think now what you have done; and tremble at it.
But I forgive thee, love. Go in and rest thee.
    SIBYLLA And he?
    DUKE   Is he not mine?
    WOLFRAM   Go in, sweet, fearlessly.   225
I come to thee, before thou'st time to feel
That I am absent.
                  [*Exeunt* SIBYLLA, ZIBA *and the Knights.*
    DUKE Wolfram, we have been friends.
    WOLFRAM   And will be ever.
I know no other way to live.
    DUKE   'Tis pity.
I would you had been one day more at sea.
    WOLFRAM   Why so?   230
    DUKE You're troublesome to-day. Have you not marked it?
    WOLFRAM Alas! that you should say so.
    DUKE   That's all needles.
Those times are past, forgotten. Hear me, knight:
That lady's love is mine. Now you know that,
Do what you dare.
    WOLFRAM   The lady! my Sibylla!   235
Oh that I did not love thee for those words,
That I might answer well.
    DUKE   Unless thou yield'st her, —
For thou hast even subdued her to thy arms,
Against her will and reason, wickedly
Torturing her soul with spells and adjurations, —   240
Unless thou giv'st her the free will again
To take her gentle course of being on,
Which flowed towards me with steady love: — O Wolfram,
Thou know'st not how she fed my soul so doing,
Even as the streams an ocean: — Give her me,   245
And we are friends again. But I forget:
Thou lovest her too; a stern, resolved rival;
And passionate, I know. Nay then, speak out:

'Twere better if we argued warmly here,
Till the blood has its way.
    WOLFRAM   Unworthy friend!   250
    DUKE Forget that I am so, and many things
Which we've been to each other, and speak out.
I would we had much wine; 'twould bring us sooner
To the right point.
    WOLFRAM   Can it be so? O Melveric!
I thought thou wert the very one of all   255
Who shouldst have heard my secret with delight.
I thought thou wert my friend.
    DUKE   All things like these,
Friendship, esteem, sympathy, hope, faith,
We need no more: away with them for ever!
Wilt follow them out of the world? Thou see'st   260
All human things die and decay around us.
'Tis the last day for us; and we stand naked
To let our cause be tried. See'st thou not why?
We love one creature: which of us shall tear her
Out of his soul? I have in all the world   265
Little to comfort me, few that do name me
With titles of affection, and but one
Who came into my soul at its night-time,
As it hung glistening with starry thoughts
Alone over its still eternity,   270
And gave it godhead. Thou art younger far,
More fit to be beloved; when thou appearest
All hearts incline to thee, all prouder spirits
Are troubled unto tears and yearn to love thee.
O, if thou knew'st thy heart-compelling power,   275
Thou wouldst not envy me the only creature
Who holds me dear. If I were such as thou,
I would not be forgetful of our friendship,
But yield to the abandoned his one joy.
    WOLFRAM Thou prob'st me to the quick. O, would
                                 to heaven, 280
That I had found thee somewhere in a battle,
Alone against the swords of twenty foes!
Then I had rescued thee, and died content,
Ignorant of the treasure I had saved thee.
But now my fate hath made a wisher of me: 285

Oh shame that it is so; and better were it
If she had never been, who is the cause!
 DUKE *He* is the cause! Oh fall the curse on him,
And may he be no more, who dares the gods
With such a wish! Speak thou no more of love,   290
No more of friendship here: the world is open:
I wish you life and merriment enough
From wealth and wine, and all the dingy glory
Fame doth reward those with, whose love-spurned hearts
Hunger for goblin immortality.   295
Live long, grow old, and honour crown thy hairs,
When they are pale and frosty as thy heart.
Away. I have no better blessing for thee.
Wilt thou not leave me?
 WOLFRAM   Should I leave thee thus?
 DUKE Why not? Or, 'cause I hate thee perfectly,   300
Must I then tell thee so? Away I pray thee.
Have I not cut all ties betwixt us off?
Why, wert thou my own soul, I'd drive thee from me.
Go, put to sea again.
 WOLFRAM   Farewell then, Duke.
Methinks thy better self indeed hath left thee,   305
And so I follow.   [*Exit.*
 DUKE Thither? Thither? Traitor
To every virtue. Then Amen is said
Unto thy time of being in this world:
Thou shalt die. Ha! the very word doth double
My strength of life: the resolution leaps   310
Into my heart divinely, as doth Mars
Upon the trembling footboard of his car;
Hurrying into battle wild and panting,
Even as my death-dispensing thought does now.
Ho! Ziba!
     Enter ZIBA
    Hush! How still, how full, how lightly   315
I move about the place since this resolve,
Like to a murder-charged thunder cloud
Stepping about the starry streets of night,
Breathless and masked,
O'er a still city sleeping by the sea.   320
Ziba, come hither; thou'rt the night I'll hang

My muffled wrath in. Come, I'll give thee business
Shall make thy life still darker, for one light on't
Must be put out. O let me joy no more,
Till Fate hath kissed my wooing soul's desire   325
Off her death-honied lips, and so set seal
To my decree, in which he's sepulchred.
Come, Ziba, thou must be my counsellor.   [*Exeunt.*

SCENE III. *The Interior of a tent.*
SIBYLLA, WOLFRAM

WOLFRAM This is the oft-wished hour, when we together
May walk upon the sea-shore: let us seek
Some greensward overshadowed by the rocks.
Wilt thou come forth? Even now the sun is setting
In the triumphant splendour of the waves.   5
Hear you not how they leap?
   SIBYLLA   Nay; we will watch
The sun go down upon a better day:
Look not on him this evening.
   WOLFRAM   Then let's wander
Under the mountain's shade in the deep valley,
And mock the woody echoes with our songs.   10
   SIBYLLA That wood is dark, and all the mountain caves
Dreadful and black, and full of howling winds:
Thither we will not wander.
   WOLFRAM   Shall we seek
The green and golden meadows, and there pluck
Flowers for thy couch, and shake the dew out of them?   15
   SIBYLLA The snake that loves the twilight is come out,
Beautiful, still, and deadly; and the blossoms
Have shed their fairest petals in the storm
Last night; the meadow's full of fear and danger.
   WOLFRAM Ah! you will to the rocky fount, and there   20
We'll see the fireflies dancing in the breeze,
And the stars trembling in the trembling water,
And listen to the daring nightingale
Defying the old night with harmony.
   SIBYLLA Nor that: but we will rather here remain,   25
And earnestly converse. What said the Duke?

Surely no good.

WOLFRAM   A few unmeaning words,
I have almost forgotten.

SIBYLLA   Tell me truly,
Else I may fear much worse.

WOLFRAM   Well: it may be
That he was somewhat angry. 'Tis no matter;   30
He must soon cool and be content.

                    Enter ZIBA

ZIBA   Hail, knight!
I bring to thee the draught of welcome. Taste it.
The Grecian sun ripened it in the grape,
Which Grecian maidens plucked and pressed; then came
The desert Arab to the palace gate,   35
And took it for his tribute. It is charmed;
And they who drink of such have magic dreams.

WOLFRAM Thanks for thy care. I'll taste it presently:
Right honey for such bees as I.

                    Enter a Knight

KNIGHT   Up, brave knight!
Arouse thee, and come forth to help and save.   40

WOLFRAM Here is my sword. Who needs it?

SIBYLLA   Is't the Duke?
O my dark Fear!

KNIGHT   'Tis he. In the wood hunting,
A band of robbers rushed on us.

WOLFRAM   How many?

KNIGHT Some twelve to five of us; and in the fight
Which now is at the hottest, my sword failed me.   45
Up then in speed, good Knight: I'll lead the way.

WOLFRAM Sibylla, what deserves he at our hands?

SIBYLLA Assist him; he preserved me.

WOLFRAM   For what end?

SIBYLLA Death's sickle points thy questions. Hesitate not,
But hence.

                    Enter a second Knight

WOLFRAM Behold another from the field —   50
Now thy news?

2nd KNIGHT   My fellow soldiers
Bleed and grow faint: fresh robbers pour upon us,
And the Duke stands at bay unhelmed against them.

WOLFRAM Brave comrade, keep the rogues before thee, dancing
At thy sword's point, but a few moments longer;   55
Then I am with thee. Farewell thou, Sibylla;
He shall not perish thus. Rise up, my men,
To horse with sword and spear, and follow me.
Where is the cup? One draught and then away:
I pledge thee, lady.   [*Takes the goblet.*
   ZIBA (*dashes it to the ground*) Out, thou villainous liquor!   60
Ha! it rings well and lies not. 'Tis right metal
For funeral bells.
   WOLFRAM   Rogue, what dost thou?
   ZIBA Pour thou unto the subterraneous gods
Libations of thy blood: I have shed wine,
Now, will ye not away?
   WOLFRAM   Come hither, slave: 65
Say, on your life, why did you spill that wine?
   ZIBA A superstitious fancy: but now hence.
'Twas costly liquor too.
   WOLFRAM   Then finish it.
'Twas well that fortune did reserve for you
These last and thickest drops here at the bottom.   70
   ZIBA Drink them? forbid the prophet!
   WOLFRAM   Slave, thou diest else.
   ZIBA Give me the beaker then. — O God, I dare not.
Death is too bitter so: alas! 'tis poisoned.
   SIBYLLA Pernicious caitiff!
   WOLFRAM   Patience, my Sibylla!
I knew it by thy lying eye. Thou'rt pardoned.   75
But for thy lord, the Saracen deal with him
As he thinks fit. Wolfram can help no murderer.
   SIBYLLA Mercy! O let me not cry out in vain:
Forgive him yet.
   WOLFRAM   The crime I have forgiven:
And Heaven, if he's forgiven there, can save him!   80
O monster! in the moment when my heart
Turned back to him with the old love again,
Then was I marked for slaughter by his hand.
I can forgive him; but no more: — lie still
Thou sworded hand, and thou be steely, heart.   85
            Enter a third Knight wounded
   3rd KNIGHT Woe! woe! Duke Melveric is the Arabs' captive.

SIBYLLA Then Heaven have mercy on him!
WOLFRAM   So 'tis best:
He was his passion's prisoner already.
    3rd KNIGHT They bind him to a column in the desart,
And aim their poisoned arrows at his heart.   90
    WOLFRAM O Melveric, why didst thou so to me?
Sibylla, I despise this savage Duke,
But thus he shall not die. No man in bonds
Can be my enemy. He once was noble:
Up once again, my men, and follow me.   95
I bring him to thee, love, or ne'er return.
    SIBYLLA A thousand tearful thanks for this. Farewell.

                                          [*Exeunt severally.*

                    SCENE IV. *A Wood*

                    MANDRAKE *and his boy*
    MANDRAKE The roots, the toadstools. That's right, and the
herbs. Now, where be the bones and the minerals?
    BOY In the other basket. Art thou in good faith, a witch?
    MANDRAKE A poor amateur. 'Tis my hobby. A philtre, a
nativity, the raising up of a paltry devil or so. I do no more.   5
Mere retail conjuring.
    BOY But what dish will thy black art stew of these simples?
    MANDRAKE With a pound of crocodile's fat we will concoct
a salve, an ointment. Thou hast heard of being invisible.
    BOY Aye, and now shall I see it? O lend me thy spectacles.   10
    MANDRAKE This is the secret: it shall be had in bottles, and
to prevent imposition all sealed with the ring of Gyges.
    BOY How shall I believe such things?
    MANDRAKE Doubt at thy peril, boy. This, I tell thee, will
make the true ointment. 'Tis no great rarity. Look for a true   15
friend, a wit who ne'er borrowed money or stole verses, a
woman without envy; there are legions of such, but they
have anointed their virtues with this pomatum till they
disappeared.
    BOY Then will I rub my warts with it. But whence have   20
you the receit?
    MANDRAKE Out of an ancient island where invisible honest
men trade with invisible money. 'Tis made according to the

law of contraries, but serves best against foibles at Court, and
there be horned beasts which use it with great comfort.   25
    BOY And wilt thou make thyself invisible?
    MANDRAKE Out, out! Who would ever lose sight of
himself? 'Tis scarce possible nowadays. Alas! 'tis a
dangerous and wicked butter, and hath so worked upon
priests' humanity, great men's wisdom, and poet's   30
immortality, that when death hath anointed us with it,
Posterity shall hold all these things for fables. But away, our
business is secret. Hear you no noise? Here come disturbers.
[Exeunt.

Enter Arabs with the DUKE

    1st ARAB Against this column: there's an ancient beast
Here in the neighbourhood, which to-night will thank us   35
For the ready meal.   [*They bind the* DUKE *against a column.*
    2nd ARAB Christian, in thy heaven
Boast that we took thy blood in recompense
Of our best comrades.
    1st ARAB   Hast a saint or mistress?
Call on them, for next minute comes the arrow.
    DUKE O Wolfram! now methinks thou lift'st the cup.   40
Strike quickly, Arab.
    1st ARAB   Brothers, aim at him.

Enter WOLFRAM and knights

    WOLFRAM Down, murderers, down.
    2nd ARAB   Fly! there are hundreds on us.
    WOLFRAM Die, ye slaves!
    [*Fight — the Arabs are part slain, part beaten off by the knights,
who pursue the flying.*
    WOLFRAM (*unbinding the* DUKE) Thank heaven, not too late!
Now you are free.
There is your life again.
    DUKE   Hast thou drunk wine?
Answer me, knight, hast thou drunk wine this evening?
    WOLFRAM Nor wine, nor poison. The slave told me all.   45
O Melveric, if I deserve it of thee,
Now canst thou mix another draught. But all
Be now forgotten and unknown to Heaven.
    DUKE And wilt thou not now kill me?
    WOLFRAM   Let us strive
Henceforward with good deeds against each other,   50

We once were friends and may be so again;
No one shall whisper of that deadly thought.
Now we will leave this coast.
     DUKE   Aye, we will step
Into a boat and steer away: but whither?
Think'st thou I'll live in the dread consciousness   55
That I have dealt so wickedly and basely,
And been of thee so like a god forgiven?
No: 'tis impossible... By your leave, friend —
                  [*Takes a sword from a fallen Arab.*
O what a coward villain must I be
So to exist.
     WOLFRAM Be patient but awhile.   60
And all these thoughts will soften.
     DUKE   The grave be patient,
That's yawning in the wood for one of us.
I want no comfort. I am comfortable,
For one of us must perish in this instant.
Fool, would thy virtue shame and crush me down;   65
And make a grateful blushing bond-slave of me?
O no! I dare be wicked still: and murderer
My thought has christened me, such I must remain.
O curse thy meek, forgiving, childish heart,
Which doth insult me with its cowardly virtue;   70
Twice-sentenced, die!   [*Strikes at* WOLFRAM.
     WOLFRAM   Madman, keep off.
     DUKE I pay my thanks in steel.   [*Fight:* WOLFRAM *falls.*
     WOLFRAM Murderer! Mayst thou never more repent —
     DUKE So then we both are blasted: but thou diest,
Who durst forgive my treachery. Now proclaim me.   75
Thy worldly work is done. I give thee leave.
          The Knights re-enter with SIBYLLA *and* ZIBA
     KNIGHT O luckless victory! our leader wounded!
     SIBYLLA Bleeding to death! and he, whom he so saved,
Armed and unhurt. O Wolfram, speak to me.
Let me not think thou'rt dying.
     WOLFRAM   But I am: 80
Slain villainously. Sibylla, had I stayed —
But thou and life are lost; so I'll be silent.
     SIBYLLA O Melveric, why kneelst thou not beside him
And weepst with me? He saved thee.

DUKE   And I've thanked him.
He'll not deny it.
    SIBYLLA   O that I could avenge thee!   85
Who did this, Wolfram?
    WOLFRAM   Thou knowest, Melveric;
At the last day reply thou to that question,
When such an Angel puts it: I'll not answer
Or then, or now.   [*Dies.*
    DUKE   Then the tale is out.
He's dead. Oh heaven, what a word for me!   90
    KNIGHT Accursed be he that did it.
    DUKE   He is cursed,
And from this moment shut up in a hell
Far from all earthly things.
    SIBYLLA   He is dead then;
Then all is dead. Speak to me never more
A word of love, pleasure or happiness.   95
My world lies with him.
    KNIGHT   All that liveth here,
Kneel down beside the body of this knight,
And swear revenge against his murderer.
    DUKE With all my heart. Methinks I'm of the dead,
And yet 'tis right so. Pray all in silence.   100
             (*They kneel. The curtain falls*)

ACT II

SCENE I. *A room in a tavern in Ancona*

ISBRAND *and other Guests drinking,* KATE *waiting on them*

ISBRAND Another flask, Kate. Thou knowest how fishy I am in my liquid delights. Dryness is akin to barrenness, and of barrenness comes nakedness and bareness, and these are melancholy, being the parables of human extremity, and of the uttermost of death and a pig's tail: therefore, good Kate, 'tis the duty of a wise man to thirst and the part of a good woman to wet his lips.

KATE Master Isbrand, the wine is sweet, but a sweet seducer. You have had three flasks, and there is morality in all trades.

ISBRAND You say true — I had forgot. There have you the morality. (*Gives her money*) Will you have history for it? Then think of that great King in Lydia, Croesus, whom they would have set on fire, but the lucky dog had seen the sun through the bottom of too many glasses, so he was too wet and went out. Will you have divinity for it? There's Bacchus, in his time a clever travelling God and an arch-Tosspot. Wilt have law? Behold my Cudgel. Poetry? Then bring the fourth bottle.

KATE 'Tis true you are not what you might be, but withal, a wellspoken customer, and the action of your right hand is too irresistible for us poor weak ones, so there's your new flask.

ISBRAND Gramercy, Hostess. This is the mystery of humanity, drank I not wine I were a tailor to-morrow; next day a dog, and in a week I should have less life than a witch's broomstick. Drinking hath been my education and my path of life. Small beer was my toothless infancy, the days of my childhood I passed in stout, porter comforted my years of Love, but my beard growing I took to sack, and now I quench the aspiration of my soul in these good wines of Hungary. And for these my merits, I hold my place at Court. — Now your health, mistress, and your lover's, my late colleague. Where is he now?

KATE The silly fellow! He would go to sea with Sir Wolfram, and of that ship we have heard nothing as yet.

A GUEST A sail has been seen this morning, and he who keeps the tower said that it was the Knight's vessel.

ISBRAND How? Then she must be in port ere this: first down with the wine, then down to the water. 40

Enter Sailors and HOMUNCULUS MANDRAKE'S *Boy*

1st SAILOR Now we're in Christendom, my lads, we'll get drunk once more. A curse on their watery superstition! those Turkish dogs do but lap the Nile. Now who would drink water that's made only to be sailed on?

2nd SAILOR Therefore wine, hostess, ale and brandy. My 45 legs hate walking on this stupid dead earth. I'm born to roll through life, and if the world won't under me tumble and toss, why, I must e'en suck up a sort of marine motion out of the can.

ISBRAND Good morrow, lusty comrades. Are you just 50 come in?

1st SAILOR Aye, at last the winds have brought our good ship, the Baris,[1] ashore.

ISBRAND The Baris that sailed in the Spring for Ægypt? What do you bring with you? 55

1st SAILOR A rare cargo. We have on board one whose body is invisible, another whose soul is in heaven's keeping, and a third, poor lady, whose life and love are shipwrecked.

ISBRAND Now first, your dead. They are my best acquaintance and my dearest gossips: your departed, who 60 is he?

BOY O mistress, let me speak, else the invisible man will be here before you know that you are not able to see him.

KATE O 'tis my Mandrake's boy. Now say who has the world lost sight of and where is thy master? 65

BOY It is even he I would tell of: in Ægypt we plundered ichneumons of their marrow, and knocked the yolks out of crocodile's eggs, with which, and all manner of mummy, he made a liniment of invisibility, and with it he swore he could anoint men out of sight. 70

ISBRAND Praised be the secrets of alchemy that can thus embody that subtlety which shall subdue the flesh and all its wickedness in an ounce of hog's lard. But is not this ointment called the fat of the land, with which those who are smeared

1 The name of Charon's boat according to Orpheus, Diod. Sic. I. 96.

do hide the hideousness of their souls so often? But go on,   75
boy, I am but a commentator on this world: to the text again.

BOY Now Mandrake had churned his bewitching butter,
potted it, and all was well: but last night in the storm, the
waves rolled, and the ship rolled in them, and in the middle
of dreams, fell the pot of balsam on the man's scull who   80
made it, broke it to pieces, and bathed him from head to foot,
and so he ran about dripping with the oil of invisibility and
tears for his lost body — but here he comes: see him not.

KATE Now will we teach thee to leave a poor woman who
loves thee to temptation and the earning of her bread, thou   85
rosicrucian fellow!

Enter MANDRAKE

ISBRAND Agreed! A game at blind man's buff. Therefore,
friends, weep no more for he is gone.

MANDRAKE I daresay that's my funeral sermon; — does he
praise me poor dear man? — and there's Kate, she weeps   90
buckets I warrant ye.

ISBRAND But weep not so, sweet Kate; 'tis true you have
lost a peerless simpleton: such flawless folly is a rich jewel
in the ring of wedlock: but add no vain tears to the waves
which roll over him.   95

MANDRAKE Sweetheart Kate, and friends all: I am not dead
nor gone, where are your eyes? I am here.

KATE O mercy! there is haunting here; did you not hear
his voice?

BOY Aye, so spake Master, but he is departed, and here is   100
no one.

MANDRAKE Good folks don't pretend any more that you
don't see me. O Lord, I am half frightened already into the
belief that I am vanished. Reasonable folks! I stand here in
the corner, by the rack of plates.   105

KATE There again! This is impudent haunting in the
daytime in a reputable house. Run and fetch Holy Water.
Alas! that my poor husband's ghost should not know that he
is dead! but he was ever absent.

ISBRAND Nay, don't be frightened, hostess: 'tis a jest of   110
mine; I have ventriloquized a little and mocked your dear
fellow's voice. Now mark you I do it again and abuse you as
if I were a ghost against my will.

MANDRAKE But Isbrand, and gentle people, can't you see

me really, not a twinkling of me? Nor my face in the pewter 115
plates? Ah, then I must be lost. But I will be seen soon and
heard and felt, rogues and hypocrites, and you shall weep
for it — or I am not Mandrake.

ISBRAND Is it not natural, comrades?

KATE Very good, but leave it, I pray you, or I shall think I 120
hear him, which is impossible, and fall a-crying which were
a waste of tears here where there are so few to see me, and
no white kerchief to hold my tears.

ISBRAND Then I will please thee, and be no more a
skeleton's prompter; but good mimic as I am you shall hear 125
a better some night, if you live after the fashion of this world;
he is called conscience and doth prattle with the voices of the
dead through the speaking trumpet of the winds. Beware of
him.

MANDRAKE Well, let me be viewless then, I am still 130
palpable, so let me cut arguments from the ash-tree, and
convince the incredulous by the aching of their shoulders
that they are short-sighted.   [*Strikes among the others.*

SAILOR Help! help! the house is falling in.

KATE Does it hail? or can you ventriloquize a cudgelling, 135
acquaintance?

BOY Murder, murder! here is the ghost of a game at single-
stick, methinks I begin to see.

ISBRAND Be patient: 'tis only electricity. — Knock again.
                              [*They fall on* MANDRAKE.
Confess, thou invisible one, is it possible for Christian eye to 140
see thee?

KATE (*striking him*) Art thou material, villain-spectre? Wilt
thou not let us mourn for my poor bridegroom,
undisturbed?

BOY If thou wilt have a voice, take this o' thy chaps. 145

MANDRAKE O gentle people! I confess. I will be invisible if
you will leave off seeing where to put your blows in; —
immaterial to keep my bones whole, and inaudible if you
will hear my petition. I am no Mandrake, I am nothing.

ISBRAND Nay, then thou hast gotten no blows, and that 150
were pity: see, I strike no longer thee — I strike nothing.

MANDRAKE Enough! I am a poor invisible man, and will
leave off haunting — But tremble, if I ever come to sight again.
                              [*Runs out, the rest after him.*

SCENE II. *The interior of a church at Ancona. The* DUKE, *in the garb of a pilgrim,* SIBYLLA *and Knights, assembled round the corpse of* WOLFRAM, *which is lying on a bier*

Dirge

If thou wilt ease thine heart
Of love and all its smart,
  Then sleep, dear, sleep;
And not a sorrow
  Hang any tear on your eyelashes;   5
    Lie still and deep,
    Sad soul, until the sea-wave washes
The rim o' th' sun to-morrow,
  In eastern sky.

But wilt thou cure thy heart   10
Of love and all its smart,
  Then die, dear, die;
'Tis deeper, sweeter,
  Than on a rose bank to lie dreaming
    With folded eye;   15
    And then alone, amid the beaming
Of love's stars, thou'lt meet her
  In eastern sky.

KNIGHT These rites completed, say your further pleasure.
  DUKE To horse and homewards in all haste: my business   20
Urges each hour. This body bury here,
With all due honours. I myself will build
A monument, whereon, in after times,
Those of his blood shall read his valiant deeds,
And see the image of the bodily nature   25
He was a man in. Scarcely dare I, lady,
Mock you with any word of consolation:
But soothing care, and silence o'er that sorrow,
Which thine own tears alone dare tell to thee
Or offer comfort for; and in all matters   30
What thy will best desires, I promise thee.
Wilt thou hence with us?
  SIBYLLA   Whither you will lead me.

My will lies there, my hope, and all my life
Which was in this world. Bring me to a nunnery:
There shall I soonest learn the way to heaven.   35
Farewell, my love, — I will not say to thee
Pale corpse, — we do not part for many days.
A little sleep, a little waking more,
And then we are together out of life.
    DUKE Cover the coffin up. This cold, calm stare   40
Upon familiar features is most dreadful:
Methinks too the expression of the face
Is changed, since all was settled gently there,
And threatens now. But I have sworn to speak
And think of that no more, which has been done. —   45
Now then into the bustle of the world!
We'll rub our cares smooth there.
    KNIGHT   This gate, my lord;
There stand the horses.
    DUKE   Then we're mounted straight.
But, pri'thee, friend, forget not that the Duke
Is still in prison: I am a poor pilgrim.   [*Exeunt.* 50
               Enter MANDRAKE
    MANDRAKE Refuge at last: Here then I am at home: I could
weep, or rather I could think that I wept, for it appears to be
but too true that I have given up the body. Well, what is, is,
and what is not, is not; and I am not what I was — for I am
what I was not; I am no more I, for I am no more: I am no   55
matter, being out of all trouble, and nobody at all, but poor
Mandrake's pure essence. And how came I to this pass?
Marry, I must either have been very sound asleep when I
died, or else I died by mistake, for I am sure I never intended
it: or else this being dead is a quite insignificant habit when   60
one's used to it: 'tis much easier than being alive, now I think
on it: only think of the trouble one has to keep up life. One
must breathe, and pass round the blood and digest and let
hair, and nails, and bone and flesh grow. — Who comes? I
dare for the sake of my skin haunt no longer.   [*Exit.* 65
      Enter ISBRAND *and* SIEGFRIED *attended*
    ISBRAND Dead and gone! a scurvy burthen to this ballad
of life. There lies he, Siegfried; my brother, and I am not
moved; dead, and I weep not. And why not, Siegfried?
    SIEGFRIED 'Tis well that you are reconciled to his lot and

your own.   70

ISBRAND Reconciled! A word out of a love tale, that's not
in my language. No, no. I am patient and still and laborious,
a good contented man; peaceable as an ass chewing a thistle;
and my thistle is revenge. I do but whisper it now: but
hereafter I will thunder the word, and I shall shoot up   75
gigantic out of this pismire shape, and hurl the bolt of that
revenge.

SIEGFRIED To the purpose: the priests return to complete
the burial.

ISBRAND Right: we are men of business here. Away with   80
the body, gently and silently; it must be buried in my duke's
chapel in Silesia: why, hereafter. (*The body is borne out by
attendants.*) That way, fellows: the hearse stands at the corner
of the square: but reverently, 'tis my brother you carry.

SIEGFRIED But the priests will discover the robbery.   85

Re-enter MANDRAKE

MANDRAKE Welcome, fellows: tell me if ye hear, whether
ye be living, or young goblins. For there is many a fellow
with broad shoulders and a goodly paunch who looks and
behaves as if he were alive, although in soul and spirit he be
three times more dead than salt fish in Lent. I, for my part,   90
am a sort of amateur goblin.

ISBRAND The very fellow for us. — What, darest thou
haunt again? Down, Sir, on your bier, and be buried as it
beseems thee.

MANDRAKE Shall I submit to be a body again? No, I am   95
above being buried. I am but a young angel, as yet
unfledged, but bye and bye I shall try a flight.

ISBRAND Lie down, lie down, vampire! or you die.

MANDRAKE Superfluous fellow, will ye be guilty of
tautology, and kill a dead man?   100

ISBRAND Down then, on the bier, and be still.

[*They throw* MANDRAKE *down on the bier and cover him with the pall.*

ISBRAND Cover thy face up if thou wilt have a good bust;
and when thou comest to the churchyard, thou mayst run if
thou must needs give death the slip: but dead thou art, and
to be buried is thy vocation. So submit.   105

Enter the Priests and bearers

SIEGFRIED A substitute in time.

ISBRAND Here come the priests: now, move not, fellow,

belie not thy destiny. — But one more farewell, Fathers; he
was my brother. (*Goes to the bier, and whispers to* MANDRAKE.)
Lie quiet, and be buried, thou ape of the dead! If thou art   110
deceased, it is thy duty; if thou art not, speak and I will
despatch thee: I hold a dagger to thy heart till thou art in the
grave. Art dead?

MANDRAKE I am, I am; I have been so all my life: bury me
in peace.   [*He is borne out, the Priests following.*   115

ISBRAND Away, we must be doing in Münsterberg: the
Governor is there, and those two Duke's sons who shall
perish for his sake. I bury my brother there: he is an
earthquake-seed, and will whisper revenge to earth, and I to
heaven; and though we whisper now, thunder shall speak   120
the word hereafter: and it shall be the thunder of the wheels
of a war-chariot in which I shall triumph like Jupiter in my
fool's cap, to fetch the Duke and his sons to Hell, and then
my bells will ring merrily, and I shall jest more merrily than
now: for I shall be Death the Court-fool. — Come, Siegfried.   125
                                                              [*Exeunt.*

MANDRAKE *runs across the stage, crying*

MANDRAKE   Who'll run a race with a ghost? Now,
Musicians, strike up Death's Hornpipe, for I dance alone
through the world like a Jack o' Lanthorn.   [*Exit.*

SCENE III. *A hall in the ducal castle of Münsterberg in the town of*
Grüssau in Silesia

TORWALD, ADALMAR, ATHULF, ISBRAND, SIEGFRIED; *the* DUKE, *disguised*
as a pilgrim; AMALA; *and other ladies and knights; conversing in various*
groups

ATHULF A fair and bright assembly: never strode
Old arched Grüssau over such a tide
Of helmed chivalry, as when to-day
Our tourney guests swept, leaping billow-like,
Its palace-banked streets. Knights shut in steel,   5
Whose shields, like water, glassed the soul-eyed maidens,
That softly did attend their armed tread,
Flower-cinctured on the temples, whence gushed down
A full libation of star-numbered tresses,
Hallowing the neck unto love's silent kiss,   10
Veiling its innocent white: and then came squires,
And those who bore war's silken tapestries,
And chequered heralds: 'twas a human river,
Brimful and beating as if the great god,
Who lay beneath it, would arise. So swings   15
Time's sea, which Age snows into and encreases,
When from the rocky side of the dim future,
Leaps into it a mighty destiny,
Whose being to endow great souls have been
Centuries hoarded, and the world meanwhile   20
Sate like a beggar upon Heaven's threshold,
Muttering its wrongs.
SIEGFRIED   My sprightly Athulf,
Is it possible that you can waste the day,
Which throws these pillared shades among such beauties,
In lonely thought?
ATHULF   Why I have left my cup,   25
A lady's lips, dropping with endless kisses,
Because your minstrels hushed their harps. Why did they?
This music, which they tickle from the strings,
Is excellent for drowning ears that gape,
When one has need of whispers.
SIEGFRIED   The old governor   30
Would have it so: his morning nap being o'er,
He'd no more need of music, but is moving

Straight to the lists.
　　ATHULF　　　　　　A curse on that mock war!
How it will shake and sour the blood, that now
Is quiet in the men! And there's my brother,　　　　　　35
Whose sword's his pleasure. A mere savage man,
Made for the monstrous times, but left out then,
Born by mistake with us.
　　ADALMAR (to ISBRAND) Be sure 'tis heavy.
One lance of mine a wolf shut his jaws on
But cracked it not, you'll see his bite upon it:　　　　40
It lies among the hunting weapons.
　　ISBRAND　　　　　　　　　　Aye,
With it I saw you once scratch out of life
A blotted Moor.
　　ADALMAR The same; it poises well,
And falls right heavy: find it.　　　　　[*Exit* ISBRAND.
　　SIEGFRIED　　　　　　　　For the tilt,
My brave lord Adalmar?
　　ATHULF　　　　　　　What need of asking?　　45
You know the man is sore upon a couch
But upright, on his bloody-hoofed steed
Galloping o'er the ruins of his foes,
Whose earthquake he hath been, there will he shout,
Laugh, run his tongue along his trembling lip,　　　　50
And swear his heart tastes honey.
　　SIEGFRIED　　　　　　　　　　Nay, thou'rt harsh;
He was the axe of Mars; but, Troy being felled,
Peace trims her bower with him.
　　ATHULF　　　　　　　　　　Aye; in her hand
He's iron still.
　　ADALMAR I care not, brother Athulf,
Whether you're right or wrong: 'tis very certain,　　55
Thank God for it, I am not Peace's lap-dog,
But Battle's shaggy whelp. Perhaps, even soon,
Good friend of Bacchus and the rose, you'll feel
Your budding wall of dalliance shake behind you,
And need my spear to prop it.
　　ATHULF　　　　　　　　Come the time!　　60
You'll see that in our veins runs brotherhood.
　　A LADY Is Siegfried here? At last! I've sought for you
By every harp and every lady's shoulder,

Not ever thinking you could breathe the air
That ducal cub of Münsterberg makes frightful   65
With his loud talk.
    SIEGFRIED   Happy in my error,
If thus to be corrected.
                    Re-enter ISBRAND
    ISBRAND   The lance, my lord:
A delicate tool to breathe a heathen's vein with.
    THE LADY What, Isbrand, thou a soldier? Fie upon thee!
Is this a weapon for a fool?   70
    ISBRAND   Madam, I pray thee pardon us. The fair have
wrested the tongue from us, and we must give our speeches
a sting of some metal — steel or gold. And I beseech thee,
lady, call me fool no longer: I grow old, and in old age you
know what men become. We are at court, and there it were   75
sin to call a thing by its right name: therefore call me a fool
no longer, for my wisdom is on the wane, and I am almost
as sententious as the governor.
    THE LADY Excellent: wilt thou become court-confessor?
    ISBRAND Aye, if thou wilt begin with thy secrets, lady. But   80
my fair mistress, and you, noble brethren, I pray you gather
around me. I will now speak a word in earnest, and hereafter
jest with you no more: for I lay down my profession of folly.
Why should I wear bells to ring the changes of your follies
on? Doth the besonneted moon wear bells, she that is the   85
parasite and zany of the stars, and your queen, ye apes of
madness? As I live I grow ashamed of the duality of my legs,
for they and the apparel, forked or furbelowed, upon them
constitute humanity; the brain no longer; and I wish I were
an honest fellow of four shins when I look into the note-book   90
of your absurdities. I will abdicate.
    THE LADY Brave! but how dispose of your dominions, most
magnanimous zany?
    ISBRAND My heirs at law are manifold. Yonder minister
shall have my jacket; he needs many colours for his deeds.   95
You shall inherit my mantle; for your sins, (be it whispered,)
chatter with the teeth for cold; and charity, which should be
their greatcoat, you have not in the heart.
    THE LADY Gramercy: but may I not beg your coxcomb for
a friend?   100
    ISBRAND The brothers have an equal claim to that crest:

they may tilt for it. But now for my crown. O cap and bells, ye eternal emblems, hieroglyphics of man's supreme right in nature; O ye, that only fall on the deserving, while oak, palm, laurel, and bay rankle on *their* foreheads, whose 105 deserts are oft more payable at the other extremity: who shall be honoured with you? Come candidates, the cap and bells are empty.

THE LADY Those you should send to England, for the bad poets and the critics who praise them. 110

ISBRAND Albeit worthy, those merry men cannot this once obtain the prize. I will yield Death the crown of folly. He hath no hair, and in this weather might catch cold and die: besides he has killed the best knight I knew, Sir Wolfram, and so is doubly deserving. Let him wear the cap, let him toll the bells; 115 he shall be our new court-fool: and, when the world is old and dead, the thin wit shall find the angel's record of man's works and deeds, and write with a lipless grin on the innocent first page for a title, 'Here begins Death's Jest-book'. — There, you have my testament: henceforth speak 120 solemnly to me, and you shall have a measured answer from me, who have relapsed into courtly wisdom.

THE LADY Come, Siegfried, let us leave this wild odd jester.
Some of us in a corner wait your music,
Your news, and stories. My lord Adalmar, 125
You must be very weary all this time,
The rest are so delighted. Come along,   [*To* SIEGFRIED
Or else his answer stuns me.

ADALMAR   Joyous creature!
Whose life's first leaf is hardly yet uncurled.

ATHULF Use your trade's language; were I journeyman 130
To Mars, the glorious butcher, I would say
She's sleek, and sacrificial flowers would look well
On her white front.

ADALMAR   Now, brother, can you think,
Stern as I am above, that in my depth
There is no cleft wherein such thoughts are hived 135
As from dear looks and words come back to me,
Storing that honey, love. O! love I do,
Through every atom of my being.

ATHULF   Aye,
So do we young ones all. In winter time

This god of butterflies, this Cupid sleeps,   140
As they do in their cases; but May comes;
With it the bee and he: each spring of mine
He sends me a new arrow, thank the boy.
A week ago he shot me for this year;
The shaft is in my stomach, and so large   145
I scarce have room for dinner.
    ADALMAR   Shall I believe thee,
Or judge mortality by this stout sample
I screw my mail o'er? Well, it may be so;
You are an adept in these chamber passions,
And have a heart that's Cupid's arrow cushion   150
Worn out with use. I never knew before
The meaning of this love. But one has taught me,
It is a heaven wandering among men,
The spirit of gone Eden haunting earth.
Life's joys, death's pangs are viewless from its bosom,   155
Which they who keep are gods; there's no paradise,
There is no heaven, no angels, no blessed spirits
No souls, or they have no eternity,
If this be not a part of them.
    ATHULF   This in a Court!
Such sort of love might Hercules have felt   160
Warm from the Hydra fight, when he had fattened
On a fresh-slain Bucentaur, roasted whole,
The heart of his pot-belly, till it ticked
Like a cathedral clock. But in good faith
Is this the very truth? Then I have found   165
My fellow fool. For I am wounded too
E'en to the quick and inmost, Adalmar.
So fair a creature! of such sweets compact
As nature stints elsewhere; which you may find
Under the tender eyelid of a serpent,   170
Or in the gurge of a kiss-coloured rose,
By drops and sparks: but when she moves, you see,
Like water from a crystal overfilled,
Fresh beauty tremble out of her and lave
Her fair sides to the ground. Of other women,   175
(And we have beauteous in this court of ours,)
I can remember whether nature touched
Their eye with brown or azure, where a vein

Runs o'er a sleeping eyelid, like some streak
In a young blossom; every grace count up,   180
Here the round turn and crevice of the arm,
There the tress-bunches, or the slender hand
Seen between harpstrings gathering music from them:
But when she leaves me I know nothing more,
(Like one from whose awakening temples rolls   185
The cloudy vision of a god away)
Than that she was divine.
    ADALMAR Fie sir, these are the spiced sighs of a heart,
That bubbles under wine; utter rhyme-gilding,
Beneath man's sober use. What do you speak of?   190
    ATHULF A woman most divine, and that I love
As you dare never.
    ADALMAR   Boy, a truce with talk.
Such words are sacred, placed within man's reach
To be used seldom, solemnly, when speaking
Of what both God and man might overhear   195
You unabashed.
    ATHULF   Of what? What is more worthy
Than the delight of youth, being so rare,
Precious, short-lived, and irrecoverable?
    ADALMAR When you do mention that adored land,
Which gives you life, pride, and security,   200
And holy rights of freedom; or in the praise
Of those great virtues and heroic men,
That glorify the earth and give it beams,
Then to be lifted by the like devotion
Would not disgrace God's angels.
    ATHULF   Well, sir, laud,   205
Worship, and swear by them, your native country
And virtues past; a phantom and a corpse:
Such airy stuff may please you. My desires
Are hot and hungry; they will have their fill
Of living dalliance, gazes, and lip-touches,   210
Or swallow up their lord. No more rebuking:
Peace be between us. For why are we brothers,
Being the creatures of two different gods,
But that we may not be each other's murderers?
    ADALMAR So be it then! But mark me,   215
I spoke not from a cold unnatural spirit,

Barren of tenderness. I feel and know
Of woman's dignity: how it doth merit
Our total being, has all mine this moment:
But they should share with us our level lives: 220
Moments there are, and one is now at hand,
Too high for them. When all the world is stirred
By some preluding whisper of that trumpet,
Which shall awake the dead, to do great things,
Then the sublimity of my affection,   225
The very height of my beloved, shows me
How far above her's glory. When you've earned
This knowledge, tell me: I will say, you love
As a man should.   *[He retires.*
    ATHULF   But this is somewhat true.
I almost think that I could feel the same   230
For her. For *her*? By heavens, 'tis Amala,
Amala only, that he so can love.
There? by her side? in conference! at smiles!
Then I am born to be a fratricide.
I feel as I were killing him. Tush, tush;   235
A phantom of my passion! But, if true —
What? What, my heart? A strangely-quiet thought,
That will not be pronounced, doth answer me.
           TORWALD *comes forward, attended by the company*
    TORWALD Break up! The day's of age. Knights to the lists,
And ladies to look on. We'll break some lances   240
Before 'tis evening. To your sports, I pray;
I follow quickly.   *[He is left alone with the* DUKE.
           Pilgrim, now your news:
Whence come you?
    DUKE   Straightway from the holy land,
Whose sanctity such floods of human blood,
Unnatural rain for it, will soon wash out.   245
    TORWALD You saw our Duke?
    DUKE   I did: but Melveric
Is strangely altered. When we saw him leap,
Shut up in iron, on his burning steed
From Grüssau's threshold, he had fifty years
Upon his head, and bore them straight and upright,   250
Through dance, and feast, and knightly tournament.
    TORWALD How is he not the same? 'Tis but three years

And a fourth's quarter past. What is the change?
A silvering of the hair? a deeper wrinkle
On cheek and forehead?
      DUKE   I do not think you'd know him,   255
Stood he where I do. No. I saw him lying
Beside a fountain on a battle-evening:
The sun was setting over the heaped plain;
And to my musing fancy his front's furrows,
With light between them, seemed the grated shadows   260
Thrown by the ribs of that field's giant, Death;
'Twixt which the finger of the hour did write
'This is the grave's'.
      TORWALD   How? Looked he sorrowful?
Knows he the dukedom's state?
      DUKE (*giving letters to* TORWALD) Ask these. He's heard
The tidings that afflict the souls of fathers;   265
How these two sons of his unfilially
Have vaulted to the saddle of the people,
And charge against him. How he gained the news,
You must know best: what countermine he digs,
Those letters tell your eyes. He bade me say,   270
His dukedom is his body, and, he forth,
That may be sleeping, but the touch of wrong,
The murderer's barefoot tread will bring him back
Out of his Eastern visions, ere this earth
Has swung the city's length.
      TORWALD   I read as much: 275
He bids me not to move; no eye to open,
But to sit still and doze, and warm my feet
At their eruption. This security
Is most unlike him. I remember oft,
When the thin harvests shed their withered grain,   280
And empty poverty yelped sour-mouthed at him,
How he would cloud his majesty of form
With priestly hangings, or the tattered garb
Of the step-seated beggar, and go round
To catch the tavern talk and the street ballad,   285
Until he knew the very nick of time,
When his heart's arrow would be on the string;
And, seizing Treason by the arm, would pour
Death back upon him.

DUKE   He is wary still,
And has a snake's eye under every leaf.   290
Your business is obedience unto him,
Who is your natal star; and mine to worm,
Leaf after leaf, into the secret volume
Of their designs. Already has our slave,
The grape juice, left the side-door of the youngest   295
Open to me. You think him innocent.
Fire flashes from him; whether it be such
As treason would consult by, or the coals
Love boils his veins on, shall through this small crevice,
In which the vine has thrust his cunning tendril,   300
Be looked and listened for.
        TORWALD   Can I believe it?
Did not I know him and his spirit's course,
Well as the shape and colour of the sun,
And when it sets and rises? Is this he?
No: 'tis the shadow of this pilgrim false,   305
Who stands up in his height of villainy,
Shadowy as a hill, and throws his hues
Of contradiction to the heavenly light,
The stronger as it shines upon him most.
Ho! pilgrim, I have weighed and found thee villain.   310
Are thy knees used to kneeling? It may chance
That thou must change the altar for the block:
Prove thou'rt his messenger.
        DUKE   Pause! I am stuffed
With an o'erwhelming spirit: press not thou,
Or I shall burst asunder, and let through   315
The deluging presence of thy duke. Prepare:
He's near at hand.
        TORWALD   Forbid it, Providence!
He steps on a plot's spring, whose teeth encircle
The throne and city.
        DUKE (*disrobing*)   Fear not. On he comes,
Still as a star robed in eclipse, until   320
The earthy shadow slips away. Who rises?
I'm changing: now who am I?
        TORWALD   Melveric!
Münsterberg, as I live and love thee!
        DUKE   Hush!

Is there not danger?
    TORWALD   Aye: we walk on ice
Over the mouth of Hell: an inch beneath us, 325
Dragon Rebellion lies ready to wake.
Ha! there behold him.
              Enter ADALMAR
    ADALMAR Lord Governor, our games are waiting for you.
Will you come with me? Base and muffled stranger,
What dost thou here? Away.
    DUKE   Prince Adalmar, 330
Where shall you see me? I will come again,
This or the next world. Thou, who carriest
The seeds of a new world, may'st understand me.
Look for me ever. There's no crack without me
In earth and all around it. Governor, 335
Let all things happen, as they will. Farewell:
Tremble for no one.
    ADALMAR   Hence! The begging monk
Prates emptily.
    DUKE   Believe him.
    TORWALD   Well, lead on;
Wert thou a king, I'd not obey thee more.   [*Exit with* ADALMAR.
    DUKE Rebellion, treason, parricidal daggers! 340
This is the bark of the court dogs, that come
Welcoming home their master. My sons too,
Even my sons! O not sons, but contracts,
Between my lust and a destroying fiend,
Written in my dearest blood, whose date run out, 345
They are become death warrants, Parricide,
And murder of the heart that loved and nourished.
Be merry, ye rich fiends! Piety's dead,
And left the world a legacy to you.
Under the green-sod are your coffins packed, 350
So thick they break each other. The day's come
When scarce a lover, for his maiden's hair,
Can pluck a stalk whose rose draws not its hue
Out of a hate-killed heart. Nature's polluted,
There's man in every secret corner of her, 355
Doing damned wicked deeds. Thou art old, world,
A hoary atheistic murderous star:
I wish that thou would'st die, or could'st be slain,

Hell-hearted bastard of the sun.
O that the twenty coming years were over!   360
Then should I be at rest, where ruined arches
Shut out the troublesome unghostly day;
And idlers might be sitting on my tomb,
Telling how I did die. How shall I die?
Fighting my sons for power; or of dotage,   365
Sleeping in purple pressed from filial veins;
And let my epitaph be, 'Here lies he,
Who murdered his two children?' Hence cursed thought!
I will enquire the purpose of their plot:
There may be good in it, and, if there be,   370
I'll be a traitor too.   [*Exit.*

SCENE IV. *A retired gallery in the ducal castle*

Enter ISBRAND *and* SIEGFRIED
ISBRAND Now see you how this dragon-egg of ours
Swells with its ripening plot? Methinks I hear
Snaky rebellion turning restless in it,
And with its horny jaws scraping away
The shell that hides it. All is ready now: 5
I hold the latch-string of a new world's wicket;
One pull — and it rolls in. Bid all our friends
Meet in that ruinous churchyard once again,
By moonrise; until then I'll hide myself;
For these sweet thoughts rise dimpling to my lips,   10
And break the dark stagnation of my features,
Like sugar melting in a glass of poison.
To-morrow, Siegfried, shalt thou see me sitting
One of the drivers of this racing earth,
With Grüssau's reins between my fingers. Ha!   15
Never since Hell laughed at the church, blood-drunken
From rack and wheel, has there been joy so mad
As that which stings my marrow now.
SIEGFRIED   Good cause,
The sun-glance of a coming crown to heat you,
And give your thoughts gay colours in the steam   20
Of a fermenting brain.
ISBRAND   Not that alone.

A sceptre is smooth handling, it is true,
And one grows fat and jolly in a chair
That has a kingdom crouching under it,
With one's name on its collar, like a dog   25
To fetch and carry. But the heart I have
Is a strange little snake. He drinks not wine
When he'd be drunk, but poison: he doth fatten
On bitter hate, not love. And oh, that duke!
My life is hate of him; and when I tread   30
His neck into the grave, I shall, methinks,
Fall into ashes with the mighty joy,
Or be transformed into a winged star:
That will be all eternal heaven distilled
Down to one thick rich minute. This sounds madly,   35
But I am mad when I remember him:
Siegfried, you know not why.
    SIEGFRIED   I never knew
That you had quarrelled.
    ISBRAND   True: but did you not see
My brother's corpse? There was a wound on't, Siegfried;
He died not gently, nor in a ripe age;   40
And I'll be sworn it was the duke that did it,
Else he had not remained in that far land,
And sent his knights to us again.
    SIEGFRIED   I thought
He was the duke's close friend.
    ISBRAND   Close as his blood:
A double-bodied soul they did appear,   45
Rather than fellow hearts.
    SIEGFRIED   I've heard it told
That they did swear and write in their best blood,
And her's they loved the most, that who died first
Should, on death's holidays, revisit him
Who still dwelt in the flesh.
    ISBRAND   O that such bond   50
Would move the jailor of the grave to open
Life's gate again unto my buried brother
But half an hour! Were I buried, like him,
There in the very garrets of the grave,
But six feet under earth (that's the grave's sky),   55
I'd jump up into life. But he's a quiet ghost;

He walks not in the churchyard after dew,
But gets to his grave betimes, burning no glow-worms,
Sees that his bones are right, and stints his worms
Most miserly. If you were murdered, Siegfried,　　　　　60
As he was by this duke, should it be so?
　　　SIEGFRIED Here speaks again your passion: what know we
Of Death's commandments to his subject-spirits,
Who are as yet the body's citizens?
What seas unnavigable, what wild forests,　　　　　65
What castles, and what ramparts there may hedge
His icy frontier?
　　　ISBRAND　　　Tower and roll what may,
There have been goblins bold who have stolen passports,
Or sailed the sea, or leaped the wall, or flung
The drawbridge down, and travelled back again.　　　　　70
So would my soul have done. But let it be.
At doomsday's dawning shall the ducal cut-throat
Wake by a tomb-fellow he little dreamt of.
Methinks I see them rising with mixed bones,
A pair of patchwork angels.
　　　SIEGFRIED　　　　　　　What does this mean?　　　　　75
　　　ISBRAND A pretty piece of kidnapping, that's all.
When Melveric's heart's heart, his new-wed wife,
Upon the bed whereon she bore these sons,
Died, as a blossom does whose inmost fruit
Tears it in twain, and in its stead remains　　　　　80
A bitter poison-berry: when she died,
What her soul left was by her husband laid
In the marriage grave, whereto he doth consign
Himself being dead.
　　　SIEGFRIED　　　Like a true loving mate.
Is not her tomb 'mid the cathedral ruins,　　　　　85
Where we to-night assemble?
　　　ISBRAND　　　　　　Say not her's:
A changeling lies there. By black night came I,
And, while a man might change two goblets' liquors,
I laid the lips of their two graves together,
And poured my brother into hers; while she,　　　　　90
Being the lightest, floated and ran over.
Now lies the murdered where the loved should be;
And Melveric the dead shall dream of heaven,

Embracing his damnation. There's revenge.
But hush! here comes one of my dogs, the princes; — 95
To work with you.   [*Exit* SIEGFRIED.
          Now for another shape;
For Isbrand is the handle of the chisels
Which Fate, the turner of men's lives, doth use
Upon the wheeling world.
          Enter ATHULF
          There is a passion
Lighting his cheek, as red as brother's hate: 100
If it be so, these pillars shall go down,
Shivering each other, and their ruins be
My step into a princedom. Doth he speak?
    ATHULF Then all the minutes of my life to come
Are sands of a great desart, into which 105
I'm banished broken-hearted. Amala,
I must think thee a lovely-faced murderess,
With eyes as dark and poisonous as nightshade;
Yet no, not so; if thou hadst murdered me,
It had been charitable. Thou hast slain 110
The love of thee, that lived in my soul's palace
And made it holy: now 'tis desolate,
And devils of abandonment will haunt it,
And call in Sins to come, and drink with them
Out of my heart. But now farewell, my love; 115
For thy rare sake I would have been a man
One story under God. Gone, gone art thou.
Great and voluptuous Sin now seize upon me,
Thou paramour of Hell's fire-crowned king,
That showedst the tremulous fairness of thy bosom 120
In heaven, and so didst ravish the best angels.
Come, pour thy spirit all about my soul,
And let a glory of thy bright desires
Play round about my temples. So may I
Be thy knight and Hell's saint for evermore. 125
Kiss me with fire: I'm thine.
    ISBRAND   Doth it run so?
A bold beginning: we must keep him up to't.
    ATHULF Isbrand!
    ISBRAND   My prince.
    ATHULF   Come to me. Thou'rt a man

I must know more of. There is something in thee,
The deeper one doth venture in thy being,   130
That drags us on and down. What dost thou lead to?
Art thou a current to some unknown sea
Islanded richly, full of syren songs
And unknown bliss? Art thou the snaky opening
Of a dark cavern, where one may converse   135
With night's dear spirits? If thou'rt one of these,
Let me descend thee.
    ISBRAND   You put questions to me
In an Egyptian or old magic tongue,
Which I can ill interpret.
    ATHULF   Passion's hieroglyphics;
Painted upon the minutes by mad thoughts,   140
Dungeoned in misery. Isbrand, answer me;
Art honest, or a man of many deeds
And many faces to them? Thou'rt a plotter,
A politician. Say, if there should come
A fellow, with his being just abandoned   145
By old desires and hopes, who would do much —
And who doth much upon this grave-paved star,
In doing, must sin much — would quick and straight,
Sword-straight and poison-quick, have done with doing;
Would you befriend him?
    ISBRAND   I can lend an arm   150
To good bold purpose. But you know me not,
And I will not be known before my hour.
Why come you here wishing to raise the devil,
And ask me how? Where are your sacrifices?
Eye-water is not his libation, prayers   155
Reach him not through earth's chinks. Bold deeds and thoughts,
What men call crimes, are his loved litany;
And from all such good angels keep us! Now sir,
What makes you fretful?
    ATHULF   I have lost that hope,
For which alone I lived. Henceforth my days   160
Are purposeless; there is no reason further
Why I should be, or should let others be;
No motive more for virtue, for forbearance,
Or anything that's good. The hourly need,
And the base bodily cravings, must be now   165

The aim of this deserted human engine.
Good may be in this world, but not for me;
Gentle and noble hearts, but not for me;
And happiness, and heroism, and glory,
And love, but none for me. Let me then wander   170
Amid their banquets, funerals, and weddings,
Like one whose living spirit is Death's Angel.
  ISBRAND What? You have lost your love and so turned sour?
And who has ta'en your chair in Amala's heaven?
  ATHULF My brother, my Cain; Adalmar.
  ISBRAND   I'll help thee, prince: 175
When will they marry?
  ATHULF I could not wish him in my rage to die
Sooner: one night I'd give him to dream hells.
To-morrow, Isbrand.
  ISBRAND   Sudden, by my life.
But, out of the black interval, we'll cast   180
Something upon the moment of their joy,
Which, should it fail to blot, shall so deform it,
That they must write it further down in time.
  ATHULF Let it be crossed with red.
  ISBRAND   Trust but to me:
I'll get you bliss. But I am of a sort   185
Not given to affections. Sire and mother
And sister I had never, and so feel not
Why sin 'gainst them should count so doubly wicked,
This side o' th' sun. If you would wound your foe,
Get swords that pierce the mind: a bodily slice   190
Is cured by surgeon's butter: let true hate
Leap the flesh wall, or fling his fiery deeds
Into the soul. So he can marry, Athulf,
And then —
  ATHULF Peace, wicked-hearted slave!
Darest thou tempt me? I called on thee for service,   195
But thou wouldst set me at a hellish work,
To cut my own damnation out of Lust:
Thou'ldst sell me to the fiend. Thou and thy master,
That sooty beast the devil, shall be my dogs,
My curs to kick and beat when I would have you.   200
I will not bow, nor follow at his bidding,
For his hell-throne. No: I will have a god

To serve my purpose; Hatred be his name;
But 'tis a god, divine in wickedness,
Whom I will worship.   [*Exit.* 205
    ISBRAND Then go where Pride and Madness carry thee:
And let that feasted fatness pine and shrink,
Till thy ghost's pinched in the tight love-lean body.
I see his life, as in a map of rivers,
Through shallows, over rocks, breaking its way,   210
Until it meet his brother's, and with that
Wrestle and tumble o'er a perilous rock,
Bare as Death's shoulder: one of them is lost,
And a dark haunted flood creeps deadly on
Into the wailing Styx. Poor Amala!   215
A thorny rose thy life is, plucked in the dew,
And pitilessly woven with these snakes
Into a garland for the King of the grave.   [*Exit.*

ACT III

SCENE I. *An apartment in the ducal castle*

The DUKE *and* TORWALD

DUKE Let them be married: give to Adalmar
The sweet society of woman's soul,
As we impregnate damask swords with odour
Pressed from young flowers' bosoms, so to sweeten
And purify war's lightning. For the other,   5
Who catches love by eyes, the court has stars,
That will take up in his tempestuous bosom
The shining place she leaves.
TORWALD   It shall be done:
The bell, that will ring merrily for their bridal,
Has but few hours to score first.
DUKE   Good. I have seen too   10
Our ripe rebellion's ringleaders. They meet
By moonrise; with them I: to-night will be
Fiends' jubilee, with heaven's spy among them.
What else was't that you asked?
TORWALD The melancholy lady you brought with you?   15
DUKE Torwald, I fear her's is a broken heart.
When first I met her in the Egyptian prison,
She was the rosy morning of a woman;
Beauty was rising, but the starry grace
Of a calm childhood might be seen in her.   20
But since the death of Wolfram, who fell there,
Heaven and one single soul only know how,
I have not dared to look upon her sorrow.
TORWALD Methinks she's too unearthly beautiful.
Old as I am, I cannot look at her,   25
And hear her voice, that touches the heart's core,
Without a dread that she will fade each instant.
There's too much heaven in her: oft it rises,
And, pouring out about the lovely earth,
Almost dissolves it. She is tender too;   30
And melancholy is the sweet pale smile,
With which she gently doth reproach her fortune.
DUKE What ladies tend her?
TORWALD   My Amala; she will not often see

One of the others.
   DUKE   Too much solitude
Maintains her in this grief. I will look to't   35
Hereafter; for the present I've enough.
We must not meet again before to-morrow.
   TORWALD I may have something to report...
   DUKE Ho! Ziba.

                    Enter ZIBA
   ZIBA   Lord of my life!
   DUKE I bought this man of Afric from an Arab,   40
Under the shadow of a pyramid,
For many jewels. He hath skill in language;
And knowledge is in him root, flower, and fruit,
A palm with winged imagination in it,
Whose roots stretch even underneath the grave,   45
And on them hangs a lamp of magic science
In his soul's deepest mine, where folded thoughts
Lie sleeping on the tombs of magi dead:
So said his master when he parted with him.
I know him skilful, faithful; take him with you;   50
He's fit for many services.
   TORWALD   I'll try him:
Wilt thou be faithful, Moor?
   ZIBA   As soul to body.
   TORWALD Then follow me. Farewell, my noble pilgrim. [*Exit.*
   DUKE It was a fascination, near to madness,
Which held me subjugated to that maiden.   55
Why do I now so coldly speak of her,
When there is nought between us? O! there is,
A deed as black as the old towers of Hell.
But hence! thou torturing weakness of remorse;
'Tis time when I am dead to think on that: 60
Yet my sun shines; so courage, heart, cheer up:
Who should be merrier than a secret villain?   [*Exit.*

SCENE II. *Another room in the same*

SIBYLLA *and* AMALA

SIBYLLA I would I were a fairy, Amala,
Or knew some of those winged wizard women,
Then I could bring you a more precious gift.
'Tis a wild graceful flower, whose name I know not;
Call it Sibylla's love, while it doth live;   5
And let it die that you may contradict it,
And say my love doth not, so bears no fruit.
Take it. I wish that happiness may ever
Flow through your days as sweetly and as still,
As did the beauty and the life to this   10
Out of its roots.
    AMALA   Thanks, my kind Sibylla:
To-morrow I will wear it at my wedding,
Since that must be.
    SIBYLLA   Art thou then discontented?
I thought the choice was thine, and Adalmar
A noble warrior worthy of his fortune.   15
    AMALA O yes: brave, honourable is my bridegroom,
But somewhat cold perhaps. If his wild brother
Had but more constancy and less insolence
In love, he were a man much to my heart.
But, as it is, I must, I will be happy;   20
And Adalmar deserves that I should love him.
But see how night o'ertakes us. Good rest, dear:
We will no more profane sleep's stillest hour.
    SIBYLLA Good night, then.   [*Exeunt.*

SCENE III. *The ruins of a spacious Gothic Cathedral and churchyard.*
On the cloister wall the Dance of Death is painted. The sepulchre of the
Dukes with massy carved folding doors, &c., by moonlight.

Enter MANDRAKE

MANDRAKE After all being dead's not so uncomfortable
when one's got into the knack of it. There's nothing to do, no
taxes to pay, nor any quarrelling about the score for ale. And
yet I begin shrewdly to suspect that death's all a take-in: as
soon as gentlemen have gained some 70 years of experience   5

they begin to be weary of the common drudgery of the
world, lay themselves down, hold their breath, close their
eyes and are announced as having entered into the fictitious
condition by means of epitaphs and effigies. But, good living
people, don't you be deceived any more: It is only a cunning   10
invention to avoid poor's rates and the reviewers. They live
all jollily underground and sneak about a little in the night
air to hear the news and laugh at their poor innocent great-
grandchildren, who take them for goblins, and tremble for
fear of death, which is at best only a ridiculous game at hide-   15
and-seek. That is my conviction, and I am quite impartial
being in the secret, but I will only keep away from the living
till I have met with a few of these gentle would-be dead, who
are shy enough, and am become initiated into their secrets,
and then I will write to the newspapers, turn King's evidence   20
and discover the whole import and secret, become more
renowned than Columbus, though sure to be opposed by the
doctors and undertakers whose invention the whole most
extravagant idea seems to be. Ah! some living folks. — Well,
I must keep up the joke a little longer, and keep away from   25
them: here are good quarters for the like of me, there I'll sleep
to-night.   [*Goes into the sepulchre.*

              Enter ISBRAND *and* SIEGFRIED
   ISBRAND Not here? That wolf-howled, witch-prayed, owl-sung
                                                          fool,
Fat mother moon hath brought the cats their light
A whole thief's hour, and yet they are not met.   30
I thought the bread and milky thick-spread lies,
With which I plied them, would have drawn to head
The state's bad humours quickly.
        SIEGFRIED   They delay
Until the twilight strollers are gone home.
        ISBRAND That may be. This is a sweet place methinks: 35
These arches and their caves, now double-nighted
With heaven's and that creeping darkness, ivy,
Delight me strangely. Ruined churches oft,
As this, are crime's chief haunt, as ruined angels
Straight become fiends. This tomb too tickleth me   40
With its wild-rose branches. Dost remember, Siegfried,
About the buried Duchess? In this cradle
I changed the new dead: here the murdered lies.

SIEGFRIED Are we so near? A frightful theft!
  ISBRAND   Fright! idiot! —
Peace; there's a footstep on the pavement.
        Enter the DUKE
           Welcome!   45
I thank you, wanderer, for coming first,
They of the town lag still.
  DUKE   The enterprise,
And you its head, much please me.
  ISBRAND   You are courteous.
  DUKE Better: I'm honest. But your ways and words
Are so familiar to my memory,   50
That I could almost think we had been friends
Since our now riper and declining lives
Undid their outer leaves.
  ISBRAND   I can remember
No earlier meeting. What need of it? Methinks
We agree well enough: especially   55
As you have brought bad tidings of the Duke.
  DUKE   If I had time,
And less disturbed thoughts, I'd search my memory
For what thou'rt like. Now we have other matters
To talk about.
  ISBRAND   And, thank the stingy star-shine,
I see the shades of others of our council.   60
   Enter ADALMAR *and other civil and military conspirators*
Though late met, well met, friends. Where stay the rest?
For we're still few here.
  ADALMAR   They are contented
With all the steps proposed, and keep their chambers
Aloof from the suspecting crowd of eyes,
Which day doth feed with sights for nightly gossip,   65
Until your hour strikes.
  ISBRAND   That's well to keep at home,
And hide, as doth Heaven's wrath, till the last minute.
Little's to say. We fall as gently on them,
As the first drops of Noah's world-washing shower
Upon the birds' wings and the leaves. Give each   70
A copy of this paper: it contains
A quick receipt to make a new creation
In our old dukedom. Here stands he who framed it.

ADALMAR The unknown pilgrim! You have warrant, Isbrand,
For trusting him?
    ISBRAND   I have.
    ADALMAR   Enough. How are the citizens?   75
You feasted them these three days.
    ISBRAND   And have them by the heart for't.
'Neath Grüssau's tiles sleep none, whose deepest bosom
My fathom hath not measured; none, whose thoughts
I have not made a map of. In the depth
And labyrinthine home of the still soul,   80
Where the seen thing is imaged, and the whisper
Joints the expecting spirit, my spies, which are
Suspicion's creeping words, have stolen in,
And, with their eyed feelers, touched and sounded
The little hiding holes of cunning thought,   85
And each dark crack in which a reptile purpose
Hangs in its chrysalis unripe for birth.
All of each heart I know.
    DUKE   O perilous boast!
Fathom the wavy caverns of all stars,
Know every side of every sand in earth,   90
And hold in little all the lore of man,
As a dew's drop doth miniature the sun:
But never hope to learn the alphabet,
In which the hieroglyphic human soul
More changeably is painted than the rainbow   95
Upon the cloudy pages of a shower,
Whose thunderous hinges a wild wind doth turn.
Know all of each! when each doth shift his thought
More often in a minute, than the air
Dust on a summer path.
    ISBRAND   Liquors can lay them: 100
Grape-juice or vein-juice.
    DUKE   Yet there may be one,
Whose misty mind's perspective still lies hid.
    ISBRAND Ha! stranger, where?
    DUKE A quiet, listening, flesh-concealed soul.
    ISBRAND Are the ghosts eavesdropping? None, that do live, 105
Listen besides ourselves.
          A struggle behind: SIEGFRIED *brings* MARIO *forward*
             Who's there?

SIEGFRIED   A fellow,
Who crouched behind the bush, dipping his ears
Into the stream of your discourse.
    ISBRAND   Come forward.
    MARIO Then lead me. Were it noon, I could not find him
Whose voice commands me: in these callous hands   110
There is as much perception for the light,
As in the depth of my poor dayless eyes.
    ISBRAND   Thy hand then.
    MARIO Art thou leader here?
    ISBRAND   Perchance.
    MARIO Then listen, as I listened unto you,
And let my life and story end together,   115
If it seem good to you. A Roman am I;
A Roman in unroman times: I've slept
At midnight in our Capitolian ruins,
And breathed the ghost of our great ancient world,
Which there doth walk: and among glorious visions, 120
That the unquiet tombs sent forth to me,
Learned I the love of Freedom. Scipio saw I
Washing the stains of Carthage from his sword,
And his freed poet, playing on his lyre
A melody men's souls replied unto: 125
Oak-bound and laurelled heads, each man a country;
And in the midst, like a sun o'er the sea
(Each helm in the crowd gilt by a ray from him),
Bald Julius sitting lonely in his car,
Within the circle of whose laurel wreath   130
All spirits of the earth and sea were spell-bound.
Down with him to the grave! Down with the god!
Stab, Cassius; Brutus, through him; through him, all!
Dead. — As he fell there was a tearing sigh:
Earth stood on him; her roots were in his heart;   135
They fell together. Caesar and his world
Lie in the Capitol; and Jove lies there,
With all the gods of Rome and of Olympus;
Corpses: and does the eagle batten on them?
No; she is flown: the owl sits in her nest;   140
The toge is cut for cowls; and falsehood dozes
In the chair of freedom, triple-crowned beast,

King Cerberus. Thence I have come in time
To see one grave for foul oppression dug,
Though I may share it.
  ISBRAND   Nay: thou'rt a bold heart. 145
Welcome among us.
  MARIO   I was guided hither
By one in white, garlanded like a bride,
Divinely beautiful, leading me softly;
And she doth place my hand in thine, once more
Bidding me guard her honour amongst men; 150
And so I will, with death to him that soils it:
For she is Liberty.
  ADALMAR   In her name we take thee;
And for her sake welcome thee brotherly.
At the right time thou comest to us, dark man,
Like an eventful unexpected night, 155
Which finishes a row of plotting days,
Fulfilling their designs.
  ISBRAND   Now then, my fellows,
No more; but to our unsuspected homes.
Good night to all who rest; hope to the watchful.
Stranger, with me. (*To* MARIO)   [*Exeunt: manet* DUKE.
  DUKE I'm old and desolate. O were I dead 160
With thee, my wife! Oft have I lain by night
Upon thy grave, and burned with the mad wish
To raise thee up to life. Thank God, whom then
I might have thought not pitiful, for lending
No ear to such a prayer. Far better were I 165
Thy grave-fellow, than thou alive with me,
Amid the fears and perils of the time.
       Enter ZIBA
Who's in the dark there?
  ZIBA   One of the dark's colour:
Ziba, thy slave.
  DUKE   Come at a wish, my Arab.
Is Torwald's house asleep yet?
  ZIBA   No: his lights still burn. 170
  DUKE Go; fetch a lantern and some working fellows
With spade and pickaxe. Let not Torwald come.
In good speed do it.   [*Exit* ZIBA.
    That alone is left me:

I will abandon this ungrateful country,
And leave my dukedom's earth behind me; all, 175
Save the small urn that holds my dead beloved:
That relic will I save from my wrecked princedom;
Beside it live and die.
     Enter TORWALD, ZIBA, *and gravediggers*
     Torwald with them!
Old friend, I hoped you were in pleasant sleep:
'Tis a late walking hour.
  TORWALD   I came to learn 180
Whether the slave spoke true. This haunted hour,
What would you with the earth? Dig you for treasure?
  DUKE Aye, I do dig for treasure. To the vault:
Lift up the kneeling marble woman there,
And delve down to the coffin. Aye, for treasure: 185
The very dross of such a soul and body
Shall stay no longer in this land of hate.
I'll covetously rake the ashes up
Of this my love-consumed incense star,
And in a golden urn, over whose sides 190
An unborn life of sculpture shall be poured,
They shall stand ever on my chamber altar.
I am not Heaven's rebel; think't not of me;
Nor that I'd trouble her sepulchral sleep
For a light end. Religiously I come 195
To change the bed of my beloved lady,
That what remains below of us may join,
Like its immortal.
  TORWALD   There is no ill here:
And yet this breaking through the walls, that sever
The quick and cold, led never yet to good. 200
  ZIBA Our work is done: betwixt the charmed moonshine
And the coffin lies nought but a nettle's shade,
That shakes its head at the deed.
  DUKE Let the men go.   [*Exeunt gravediggers.*
     Now Death, thou shadowy miser,
I am thy robber; be not merciful, 205
But take me in requital. There she is then;
I cannot hold my tears, thinking how altered.
O thoughts, ye fleeting, unsubstantial things,
Thou formless, viewless, and unsettled memory!

How dare ye yet survive that gracious image,   210
Sculptured about the essence whence ye rose?
That words of hers should ever dwell in me,
Who is as if she never had been born
To all earth's millions, save this one! Nay, prithee,
Let no one comfort me. I'll mourn awhile   215
Over her memory.
    TORWALD   Let the past be past,
And Lethe freeze unwept on over it.
What is, be patient with; and, with what shall be,
Silence the body-bursting spirit's yearnings.
Thou say'st that, when she died, that day was spilt   220
All beauty flesh could hold; that day went down
An oversouled creation. The time comes
When thou shalt find again thy blessed love,
Pure from all earth, and with the usury
Of her heaven-hoarded charms.
    DUKE   Is this the silence   225
That I commanded? Fool, thou say'st a lesson
Out of some philosophic pedant's book.
I loved no desolate soul: she was a woman,
Whose spirit I knew only through those limbs,
Those tender members thou dost dare despise;   230
By whose exhaustless beauty, infinite love,
Trackless expression only, I did learn
That there was aught yet viewless and eternal;
Since they could come from such alone. Where is she?
Where shall I ever see her as she was?   235
With the sweet smile, she smiled only on me;
With those eyes full of thoughts, none else could see?
Where shall I meet that brow and lip with mine?
Hence with thy shadows! But her warm fair body,
Where's that? There, mouldered to the dust. Old man   240
If thou dost dare to mock my ears again
With thy ridiculous, ghostly consolation,
I'll send thee to the blessings thou dost speak of.
    TORWALD For Heaven's and her sake restrain this passion.
    DUKE She died. But Death is old and half worn out: 245
Are there no chinks in't? Could she not come to me?
Ghosts have been seen; but never in a dream,
After she'd sighed her last, was she the blessing

Of these desiring eyes. All, save my soul,
And that but for her sake, were his who knew   250
The spell of Endor, and could raise her up.
    TORWALD   Another time that thought were impious.
Unreasonable longings, such as these,
Fit not your age and reason. In sorrow's rage
Thou dost demand and bargain for a dream,   255
Which children smile at in their tales.
    ZIBA   Smile ignorance!
But, sure as men have died, strong necromancy
Hath set the clock of time and nature back;
And made Earth's rooty, ruinous, grave-piled caverns
Throb with the pangs of birth. Aye, were I ever   260
Where the accused innocent did pray
The dead, whose murder he was falsely charged with,
To rise and speak him free, I would essay
My sires' sepulchral magic.
    DUKE   Slave, thou tempt'st me
To lay my sword's point to thy throat, and say   265
'Do it or die thyself'.
    TORWALD   Prithee, come in.
To cherish hopes like these is either madness,
Or a sure cause of it. Come in and sleep:
To-morrow we'll talk further.
    DUKE   Go in thou.
Sleep blinds no eyes of mine, till I have proved   270
This slave's temptation.
    TORWALD   Then I leave you to him.
Good night again.   [*Exit* TORWALD.
    DUKE   Good night, and quiet slumbers.
Now then, thou juggling African, thou shadow,
Think'st thou I will not murder thee this night,
If thou again dare tantalize my soul   275
With thy accursed hints, thy lying boasts?
Say, shall I stab thee?
    ZIBA   Then thou murder'st truth.
I spoke of what I'd do.
    DUKE   You told ghost-lies,
And thought I was a fool because I wept.
Now, once more, silence: or to-night I shed   280
Drops royaller and redder than those tears.

Enter ISBRAND *followed by* SIEGFRIED *with wine, &c.*
ISBRAND Pilgrim, not yet abed? Why, ere you've time
To lay your cloak down, heaven will strip off night,
And show her daily bosom.
DUKE   Sir, my eyes
Never did feel less appetite for sleep: 285
I and my slave intend to watch till morrow.
ISBRAND Excellent. You're a fellow of my humour.
I never sleep o' nights; the black sky likes me,
And the soul's solitude, while half mankind
Lies quiet in earth's shade rehearsing death.   290
Come, let's be merry: I have sent for wine,
And here it comes. These mossy stones about us
Will serve for stools, although they have been turrets
Which scarce aught touched but sunlight, or the claw
Of the strong-winged eagles, who lived here   295
And fed on battle-bones. Come sit, sir stranger;
Sit too, my devil-coloured one; here's room
Upon my rock. Fill, Siegfried.
SIEGFRIED   Yellow wine,
And rich be sure. How like you it?
DUKE Better ne'er wetted lip.   300
ISBRAND Then fill again. Come, hast no song to-night,
Siegfried? Nor you, my midnight of a man?
I'm weary of dumb toping.
SIEGFRIED   Sing, yourself, Sir.
My songs are staler than the cuckoo's tune:
And you, companions?
DUKE   We are quite unused.   305
ISBRAND Then you shall have a ballad of my making.
SIEGFRIED How? do you rhyme too?
ISBRAND Sometimes, in leizure moments
And a romantic humour; this I made
One night a-strewing poison for the rats   310
In the kitchen corner.
DUKE   And what's your tune?
ISBRAND What is the night-bird's tune, wherewith she startles
The bee out of his dream and the true lover,
And both in the still moonshine turn and kiss
The flowery bosoms where they rest, and murmuring   315
Sleep smiling and more happily again?

What is the lobster's tune when he is boiled?
I hate your ballads that are made to come
Round like a squirrel's cage, and round again.
We nightingales sing boldly from our hearts: 320
So listen to us.
                    Song by ISBRAND
            Squats on a toad-stool under a tree
                A bodiless childfull of life in the gloom,
            Crying with frog voice, 'What shall I be?
            Poor unborn ghost, for my mother killed me   325
                Scarcely alive in her wicked womb.
            What shall I be? shall I creep to the egg
                That's cracking asunder yonder by Nile,
                    And with eighteen toes,
                    And a snuff-taking nose,   330
                Make an Egyptian crocodile?
            Sing, "Catch a mummy by the leg
            And crunch him with an upper jaw,
            Wagging tail and clenching claw;
            Take a bill-full from my craw,   335
            Neighbour raven, caw, O caw,
            Grunt, my crocky, pretty maw!"

            'Swine, shall I be one? 'Tis a dear dog;
                But for a smile, and kiss, and pout,
            I much prefer *your* black-lipped snout,   340
                    Little, gruntless, fairy hog,
                    Godson of the hawthorn hedge.
                For, when Ringwood snuffs me out,
                    And 'gins my tender paunch to grapple,
                Sing, "'Twixt your ancles visage wedge,   345
                    And roll up like an apple."

            'Serpent Lucifer, how do you do?
            Of your worms and your snakes I'd be one or two
                For in this dear planet of wool and of leather
            'Tis pleasant to need no shirt, breeches or shoe, 350
                And have arm, leg, and belly together.
                Then aches your head, or are you lazy?
                Sing, "Round your neck your belly wrap,
                Tail-a-top, and make your cap

Any bee and daisy."   355

'I'll not be a fool, like the nightingale
Who sits up all midnight without any ale,
    Making a noise with his nose;
Nor a camel, although 'tis a beautiful back;
Nor a duck, notwithstanding the music of quack   360
    And the webby, mud-patting toes.
I'll be a new bird with the head of an ass,
    Two pigs' feet, two men's feet, and two of a hen;
Devil-winged; dragon-bellied; grave-jawed, because grass
    Is a beard that's soon shaved, and grows seldom again 365
        Before it is summer; so cow all the rest;
        The new Dodo is finished. O! come to my nest.'

SIEGFRIED A noble hymn to the belly gods indeed:
Would that Pythagoras heard thee, boy!
    ISBRAND I fear you flatter: 'tis perhaps a little   370
Too sweet and tender, but that is the fashion;
Besides my failing is too much sentiment.
Fill the cups up, and pass them round again;
I'm not my nightly self yet. There's creation
In these thick yellow drops. By my faith, Siegfried,   375
A man of meat and water's a thin beast,
But he who sails upon such waves as these
Begins to be a fellow. The old gods
Were only men and wine.
    SIEGFRIED   Here's to their memory.
They're dead, poor sinners, all of them but Death,   380
Who has laughed down Jove's broad, ambrosian brow,
Furrowed with earthquake frowns: and not a ghost
Haunts the gods' town upon Olympus' peak.
    ISBRAND Methinks that earth and heaven are grown bad
                                                    neighbours,
And have blocked up the common door between them.   385
Five hundred years ago had we sat here
So late and lonely, many a jolly ghost
Would have joined company.
    SIEGFRIED   To trust in story,
In the old times Death was a feverish sleep,
In which men walked. The other world was cold   390

And thinly-peopled, so life's emigrants
Came back to mingle with the crowds of earth:
But now great cities are transplanted thither,
Memphis, and Babylon, and either Thebes,
And Priam's towery town with its one beech. 395
The dead are most and merriest: so be sure
There will be no more haunting, till their towns
Are full to the garret; then they'll shut their gates,
To keep the living out, and perhaps leave
A dead or two between both kingdoms.
    DUKE   Ziba; 400
Hear'st thou, phantastic mountebank, what's said?
    ZIBA Nay: as I live and shall be one myself,
I can command them hither.
    ISBRAND   Whom?
    ZIBA   Departed spirits.
    DUKE He who dares think that words of human speech,
A chalky ring with monstrous figures in it, 405
Or smoky flames can draw the distant souls
Of those, whose bones and monuments are dust,
Must shudder at the restless, broken death,
Which he himself in age shall fall into.
    ISBRAND Suppose we four had lived in Cyrus' time, 410
And had our graves under Egyptian grass,
D'you think, at whistling of a necromant,
I'd leave my wine or subterranean love
To know his bidding? Mummies cannot pull
The breathing to them, when they'd learn the news. 415
    ZIBA Perhaps they do, in sleep, in swoons, in fevers:
But your belief's not needed.
                  (*To the* DUKE) You remember
The damsel dark at Mecca, whom we saw
Weeping the death of a pale summer flower,
Which her spear-slain beloved had tossed to her 420
Galloping into battle?
    DUKE   Happy one!
Whose eyes could yield a tear to soothe her sorrows.
But what's that to the point?
    ZIBA   As those tears fell,
A magic scholar passed; and, their cause known,
Bade her no longer mourn: he called a bird, 425

And bid it with its bill select a grain
Out of the gloomy deathbed of the blossom.
The feathery bee obeyed; and scraped aside
The sand, and dropped the seed into its grave:
And there the old plant lay, still and forgotten,   430
By its just budding grandsons; but not long:
For soon the floral necromant brought forth
A wheel of amber, (such may Clotho use
When she spins lives,) and as he turned and sung,
The mould was cracked and shouldered up: there came   435
A curved stalk, and then two leaves unfurled,
And slow and straight between them there arose,
Ghostlily still, again the crowned flower.
Is it not easier to raise a man,
Whose soul strives upward ever, than a plant,   440
Whose very life stands halfway on death's road,
Asleep and buried half?
　　　DUKE   This was a cheat:
The herb was born anew out of a seed,
Not raised out of a bony skeleton.
What tree is man the seed of?
　　　ZIBA   Of a ghost;   445
Of his night-coming, tempest-waved phantom:
And even as there is a round dry grain
In a plant's skeleton, which being buried
Can raise the herb's green body up again;
So is there such in man, a seed-shaped bone,   450
Aldabaron, called by the Hebrews Luz,
Which, being laid into the ground, will bear
After three thousand years the grass of flesh,
The bloody, soul-possessed weed called man.
　　　ISBRAND Let's have a trick then in all haste, I prithee.   455
The world's man-crammed; we want no more of them:
But show me, if you will, some four-legged ghost;
Rome's mother, the she-wolf; or the fat goat
From whose dugs Jove sucked godhead; any thing;
Pig, bullock, goose; for they have goblins too,   460
Else ours would have no dinner.
　　　ZIBA   Were you worthy,
I'd raise a spirit whom your conscience knows;
And he would drag thee down into that world,

Whither thou didst send him.
    ISBRAND   Thanks for the offer.
Our wine's out, and these clouds, whose blackest wombs   465
Seem swelling with a second centaur-birth,
Threaten plain water. So good night.   [*Exit with* SIEGFRIED.
    DUKE Obstinate slave! Now that we are alone,
Durst thou again say life and soul has lifted
The dead man from the grave, and sent him walking   470
Over the earth?
    ZIBA   I say it, and will add
Deed to my word, not oath. Within what tomb
Dwells he, whom you would call?
    DUKE   There. But stand off!
If you do juggle with her holy bones,
By God I'll murder thee. I don't believe you,   475
For here next to my heart I wear a bond,
Written in the blood of one who was my friend,
In which he swears that, dying first, he would
Borrow some night his body from the ground,
To visit me once more. One day we quarrelled,   480
Swords hung beside us and we drew: he fell.
Yet never has his bond or his revenge
Raised him to my bed-side, haunting his murderer
Or keeping blood-sealed promise to his friend.
Does not this prove you lie?
    ZIBA   'Tis not my spell: 485
Shall I try that with him?
    DUKE   Never on him.
The heavy world press on him, where he lies,
With all her towers and mountains!
    ZIBA   Listen, lord.
Time was when Death was young and pitiful,
Though callous now by use; and then there dwelt,   490
In the thin world above, a beauteous Arab,
Unmated yet and boyish. To his couch
At night, which shone so starry through the boughs,
A pale flower-breathed nymph with dewy hair
Would often come, but all her love was silent;   495
And ne'er by daylight could he gaze upon her,
For ray by ray, as morning came, she paled,
And like a snow of air, dissolved i' th' light,

Leaving behind a stalk with lilies hung,
Round which her womanish graces had assembled.   500
So did the early love-time of his youth
Pass with delight: but when, compelled at length,
He left the wilds and woods for riotous camps
And cities full of men, he saw no more,
Tho' prayed and wept for, his old bed-time vision,   505
The pale dissolving maiden. He would wander
Sleepless about the waste benighted fields,
Asking the speechless shadows of his thoughts
'Who shared my couch? Who was my love? Where is she?'
Thus passing through a grassy burial-ground,   510
Wherein a new-dug grave gaped wide for food,
'Who was she?' cried he, and the earthy mouth
Did move its nettle-bearded lips together,
And said, ''Twas I — Death: behold our child!'
The wanderer looked, and on the lap of the pit   515
A young child slept as at a mother's breast.
He raised it and he reared it. From that infant
My race, the death-begotten, draw their blood:
Our prayer for the diseased works more than medicine;
Our blessings oft secure grey hairs and happy   520
To new-born infants; and, in case of need,
The dead and gone are re-begotten by us,
And motherlessly born to second life.
    DUKE I've heard your tale. Now exorcise: but mark!
If thou dost dare to make my heart thy fool,   525
I'll send thee to thy grave-mouthed grandam, Arab.
    ZIBA Wilt thou submit unmurmuring to all evils,
Which this recall to a forgotten being
May cause to thee and thine?
    DUKE   With all my soul,
So I may take the good.
    ZIBA   And art thou ready   530
To follow, if so be its will, the ghost,
Whom you will re-imbody, to the place
Which it doth now inhabit?
    DUKE   My first wish.
Now to your sorcery: and no more conditions,
In hopes I may break off. All ill be mine,   535
Which shall the world revisit with the being

That lies within.
    ZIBA   Enough. Upon this scroll
Are written words, which read, even in a whisper,
Would in the air create another star;
And, more than thunder-tongued storms in the sky,   540
Make the old world to quake and sweat with fear;
And, as the chilly damps of her death-swoon
Fall and condense, they to the moon reflect
The forms and colours of the pale old dead.
Laid there among the bones, and left to burn   545
With sacred spices, its keen vaporous power
Would draw to life the earliest dead of all.
Swift as the sun doth ravish a dew-drop
Out of a flower. But see, the torch goes out:
How shall I light it?
    DUKE   Here's my useless blood-bond;   550
These words, that should have waked illumination
Within a corpse's eyes, will make a tinder,
Whose sparks might be of life instead of fire.
Burn it.
    ZIBA An incense for thy senses, god of those,
To whom life is as death to us; who were,   555
Ere our grey ancestors wrote history;
When these our ruined towers were in the rock;
And our great forests, which do feed the sea
With storm-souled fleets, lay in an acorn's cup:
When all was seed that now is dust; our minute   560
Invisibly far future. Send thy spirit
From plant of the air, and from the air and earth,
And from earth's worms, and roots, again to gather
The dispersed being, 'mid whose bones I place
The words which, spoken, shall destroy death's kingdom,   565
And which no voice, but thunder, can pronounce.
Marrow fill bone, and vine-like veins run round them,
And flesh, thou grass, mown wert thou long ago —
Now comes the brown dry after-crop. Ho! ghost!
There's thy old heart a-beating, and thy life   570
Burning on the old hearth. Come home again!
    DUKE Hush! Do you hear a noise?
    ZIBA   It is the sound
Of the ghost's foot on Jacob's ladder-rungs.

DUKE More like the tread upon damp stony steps
Out of a dungeon. Dost thou hear a door   575
Drop its great bolt and grate upon its hinges?
   ZIBA (*aside*) Serpentine Hell! That is thy staircase echo,
And thy jaws' groaning. What betides it?
   DUKE Thou human murder-time of night,
What hast thou done?   580
   ZIBA My task: give me death if the air has not
What was the earth's but now. Ho there! i' th' vault.
   A VOICE Who breaks my death?
   ZIBA Draw on thy body, take up thy old limbs,
And then come forth tomb-born.   585
   MANDRAKE (*within*) I have drawn on my stockings, and
taken up my old jerkin: but before I go out, can't you give
me some water to shave with? I have a beard of a week's
growth with which I decline appearing before the ladies; and
on an occasion of being raised one would willingly be a little   590
spruce, master Sorcerer.
   DUKE One moment's peace and silence!
Let me remember what a grace she had,
Even in her dying hour: her soul set not,
But at its noon Death like a cloud came o'er it,   595
And now hath passed away. O come to me
Thou dear departed spirit of my wife;
And, surely as I clasp thee once again,
Thou shalt not die without me.
   ZIBA   Ho! there, Grave,
Is life within thee?   600
   A VOICE *from within* Melveric, prepare.
   MANDRAKE *from within* Coming, coming!
This cursed boot!
   DUKE Did'st hear that answer? Open, and let in
The blessing to my eyes, whose subtle breath   605
Doth penetrate my heart's quick; let me hear
That dearest name out of those dearest lips.
Who's there? Who comes?
   ZIBA   Momus of Hell, what's this?
              Enter MANDRAKE *from the Sepulchre*
   MANDRAKE A poor ghost of one Homunculus Mandrake,
Apothecary, often called by the boys in the street, Monkey   610
Drake, at your service. Excuse my disorder. And, conjurer,

I'll give you a little bit of advice: the next time don't bait your
ghost-trap with bombast and doggrell, but good beef: we
live poorly in the dead line: and so I'll promise you, you may
catch as many ghosts, if they are of one mind with my   615
stomach, in a night in this churchyard, as rats in a granary.
But your commands, gentlemen.

    DUKE Is this thy wretched jest, thou villainous fool?
But I will punish thee, by heaven, and thou too
Shalt soon be what thou shouldst have better acted.   620

    MANDRAKE Excuse me. As you have thought proper to call
me to the living, I shall take the liberty of remaining alive. I
am more used to it; and living was ever my hobby. If you
want to speak to another ghost of longer standing, look into
the old lumber room of a vault again. Some one seems to be   625
putting himself together there: or advertise for a ghost; for
my part, I was always dead against my will, and shall write
an Essay on it to be dedicated to my black friend here: good
night, gentlemen. I must vanish, for I must go to Egypt once
more to make the salve again: and this time I shall pot it in   630
tin. Old Sir, you must not take it ill, if I offend you: we dead
are odd fish. Good night, all.   [*Exit.*

    DUKE Thou disappointed cheat! Was this a fellow,
Whom thou hadst hired to act a ghostly part?
Thou see'st how well he does it. But away!   635
Or I will teach thee better to rehearse it.

    ZIBA Death is a hypocrite, a white dissembler,
Like all that doth seem good! I am put to shame.   [*Exit.*

    DUKE Deceived and confounded vain desires!
Why laugh I not, and ridicule myself?   640
Come, I will leave this chilly silent place,
For nothing's to be gained by waiting in it.
'Tis still, and cold, and nothing in the air
But an old grey twilight, or of eve or morn
I know not which, dim as futurity,   645
And sad and hoary as the ghostly past,
Fills up the space. Hush! not a wind is there,
Not a cloud sails over the battlements,
Not a bell tolls the hour. Is there an hour?
Or is not all gone by, which here did hive,   650
Of men and their life's ways? If I could but hear
The ticking of a clock, or some one breathing,

Or e'en a cricket's chirping, or the grating
Of the old gates amidst the marble tombs,
I should be sure that this was still the world.   655
Hark! Hark! Doth nothing stir?
No light, and still no light, besides this ghost
That mocks the dawn, unaltered? Still no sound?
No voice of man? No cry of beast? No rustle
Of any moving creature? And sure I feel   660
That I remain the same: no more round blood-drops
Roll joyously along my pulseless veins:
The air I seem to breathe is still the same:
And the great dreadful thought, that now comes o'er me,
Must remain ever as it is, unchanged. —   665
This moment doth endure for evermore;
Eternity hath overshadowed time;
And I alone am left of all that lived,
Pent in this narrow, horrible conviction.
Ha! the dead soon will wake! My Agnes, rise;   670
Rise up, my wife! One look, ere Wolfram comes;
Quick, or it is too late: the murdered hasten: [*Exit.*
My best-beloved, come once to my heart...
But ah! who art thou?
   The gates of the sepulchre fly open and discover WOLFRAM.
 WOLFRAM   Wolfram, murderer,
To whose heart thou didst come with horrid purpose.   675
 DUKE Lie of my eyes, begone! Are thou not dead?
Are not the worms, that ate thy marrow, dead?
What dost thou here, thou wretched goblin fool?
Think'st thou, I fear thee? Thou man-mocking air,
Thou art not truer than a mirror's image,   680
Nor half so lasting. Back again to coffin,
Thou baffled idiot spectre, or haunt cradles:
Or stay, and I'll laugh at thee. Guard thyself,
If thou pretendest life.
 WOLFRAM Is this thin air, that thrusts thy sword away?
Flesh, bones, and soul, and blood that thou stol'st from me,   685
Upon thy summons, bound by bloody signs,
Here Wolfram stands: what wouldst thou?
 DUKE   What paper else,
But that cursed compact, could have made full Hell
Boil over, and spill thee, thou topmost damned?

But down again! I'll see no more of thee. 690
Hound, to thy kennel! to your coffin, bones!
Ghost, to thy torture!
    WOLFRAM   Thou returnest with me;
So make no hurry. I will stay awhile
To see how the world goes, feast and be merry,
And then to work again.
    DUKE   Darest thou stand there, 695
Thou shameless spirit, and assert thyself,
While I defy, and question, and deride thee?
The stars, I see them dying: clearly all
The passage of this night remembrance gives me,
And I think coolly: but my brain is mad, 700
Else why behold I that? Is't possible
Thou'rt true, and worms have vomited thee up
Upon this rind of earth? No; thou shalt vanish.
Was it for this I hated thee and killed thee?
I'll have thee dead again, and hounds and eagles 705
Shall be thy graves, since this old, earthy one
Hath spat thee out for poison.
    WOLFRAM   Thou, old man,
Art helpless against me. I shall not harm thee;
So lead me home. I am not used to sunlight,
And morn's a-breaking.
    DUKE   Then there is rebellion 710
Against all kings, even Death. Murder's worn out
And full of holes; I'll never make't the prison,
Of what I hate, again. Come with me, spectre;
If thou wilt live against the body's laws,
Thou murderer of Nature, it shall be 715
A question, which haunts which, while thou dost last.
So come with me.   [*Exeunt.*

ACT IV

SCENE I. *An apartment in the Governor's palace*

The DUKE *and an attendant*

DUKE Your lord sleeps yet?

ATTENDANT   An hour ago he rose:
About this time he's busy with his falcons,
And then he takes his meal.

DUKE   I'll wait for him. [*Exit Attendant.*
How strange it is that I can live to-day;
Nay look like other men, who have been sleeping   5
On quiet pillows and not dreamt! Methinks
The look of the world's a lie, a face made up
O'er graves and fiery depths; and nothing's true
But what is horrible. If man could see
The perils and diseases that he elbows,   10
Each day he walks a mile; which catch at him,
Which fall behind and graze him as he passes;
Then would he know that Life's a single pilgrim,
Fighting unarmed amongst a thousand soldiers.
It is this infinite invisible   15
Which we must learn to know, and yet to scorn,
And, from the scorn of that, regard the world
As from the edge of a far star. Now then
I feel me in the thickest of the battle;
The arrow-shower pours down, swords hew, mines open   20
Their ravenous mouths about me; it rains death
But cheerly I defy the braggart storm,
And set my back against a rock, to fight
Till I am bloodily won.

Enter TORWALD

TORWALD   How? here already?
I'm glad on't, and to see you look so clear   25
After that idle talk. How did it end?

DUKE Scarcely as I expected.

TORWALD   Dared he conjure?
But surely you have seen no ghost last night:
You seem to have supped well and slept.

DUKE   We'd wine,
And some wild singing. Of the necromancy   30

We'll speak no more. Ha! Do you see a shadow?
    TORWALD Aye: and the man who casts it.
    DUKE 'Tis true; my eyes are dim and dull with watching.
This castle that fell down, and was rebuilt
With the same stones, is the same castle still;   35
And so with him.
Enter WOLFRAM
    TORWALD   What mean you?
    DUKE   Impudent goblin!
Darest thou the daylight? Dar'st be seen of more
Than me, the guilty? Vanish! Though thou'rt there,
I'll not believe I see thee.
    TORWALD   Who's the stranger?
You speak as one familiar.
    DUKE   Is aught here   40
Besides ourselves? I think not.
    TORWALD   Yet you gaze
Straight on the man.
    DUKE   A villainous friend of mine;
Of whom I must speak well, and still permit him
To follow me. — So thou'rt yet visible,
Thou grave-breaker! If thou wilt haunt me thus,   45
I'll make thee my fool, ghost, my jest and zany. —
'Tis his officious gratitude that pains me:
The carcase owes to me its ruinous life,
(Between whose broken walls and cloven sides
You see the other world's grey spectral light;)   50
Therefore he clings to me so ivily. —
Now, goblin, lie about it. — 'Tis in truth
A faithful slave.
    WOLFRAM   If I had come unsummoned,
If I had burst into your sunny world,
And stolen visibility and birth   55
Against thy prayers, thus shouldst thou speak to me:
But thou hast forced me up, remember that.
I am no fiend, no foe; then let me hear
These stern and tyrannous rebukes no more.
Wilt thou be with the born, that have not died?   60
I vanish: now a short farewell. I fade;
The air doth melt me, and, my form being gone,
I'm all thou see'st not.   [*Exit.*

DUKE Dissolved like snow in water! Be my cloud,
My breath, and fellow soul, I can bear all,   65
As long as thou art viewless to these others. —
Now there are two of us. How stands the bridal?
TORWALD This evening 'twill be held.
DUKE   Good; and our plot
Leaps on your pleasure's lap; here comes my gang;
Away with you.   [*Exit* TORWALD.
                    I do begin to feel   70
As if I were a ghost among the men,
As all I loved are; for their affections
Hang on things new, young, and unknown to me:
And that I am is but the obstinate will
Of this my hostile body.   75
          Enter ISBRAND, ADALMAR, *and* SIEGFRIED
ISBRAND Come, let's be doing: we have talked whole nights
Of what an instant, with one flash of action,
Should have performed: you wise and speaking people
Need some one, with a hatchet-stroke, to free
The Pallas of your Jove-like headaches.
DUKE   Patience: 80
Fledging comes after hatching. One day more:
This evening is the wedding of the prince,
And with it feasts and maskings. In mid bowls
And giddy dances let us fall upon them.
SIEGFRIED Well thought: our enemies will be assembled.   85
ISBRAND I like to see Ruin at dinner time,
Firing his cannons with the coals they lit
To boil the flesh-pots on. But what say you
To what concerns you most?   [*To* ADALMAR.
ADALMAR   That I am ready
To hang my hopeful crown of happiness   90
Upon the temple of the public good.
ISBRAND Of that no need. Your wedding shall be finished;
Or left, like a full goblet yet untasted,
To be drunk up with greater thirst from toil.
I'll wed too when I've time. My honest pilgrim,   95
The melancholy lady, you brought with you,
Looks on me with an eye of much content:
I have sent some rhymed love-letters unto her,
In my best style. D'you think we're well matched?

ADALMAR How? The lion to thirst after the bee's dew? 100
ISBRAND True: I am rough, a surly bellowing storm;
But fallen, never tear did hang more tender
Upon the eyelash of a love-lorn girl,
Or any Frenchman's long, frost-bitten nose,
Than in the rosecup of that lady's life 105
I shall lie trembling. Pilgrim, plead for me
With a tongue love-oiled.
DUKE   Win her, sir, and wear her.
But you and she are scarcely for one world.
ISBRAND Enough; I'll wed her. Siegfried, come with me;
We'll talk about it in the rainy weather. 110
Pilgrim, anon I find you in the ruins,
Where we had wine last night.   [*Exit with* SIEGFRIED.
ADALMAR Would that it all were over, and well over!
Suspicions flash upon me here and there:
But we're in the mid ocean without compass, 115
Winds wild, and billows rolling us away:
Onwards with hope!
DUKE   Of what? Youth, is it possible
That thou art toiling here for liberty,
And others' welfare, and such virtuous shadows
As philosophic fools and beggars raise 120
Out of the world that's gone? Thou'lt sell thy birthright
For incense praise, less tickling to the sense
Than Esau's pottage steam?
ADALMAR   No, not for these,
Fame's breath and praise, its shadow. 'Tis my manner
To do what's right and good.
DUKE   Thou'rt a strange prince. 125
Why all the world, except some fifty lean ones,
Would, in your place and at your ardent years,
Seek the delight that lies in woman's limbs
And mountain-covering grapes. What's to be royal,
Unless you pick those girls, whose cheeks you fancy, 130
As one would cowslips? And see hills and valleys
Mantled in autumn with the snaky plant,
Whose juice is the right madness, the best heaven?
Have men, and beasts, and woods, with flowers and fruit
From all the earth, one's slaves; bid the worm eat 135
Your next year's purple from the mulberry leaf,

The tiger shed his skin to line your robes,
And men die, thousands in a day, for glory?
Such things should kings bid from their solitude
Upon the top of Man. Justice and Good,   140
All penniless, base, earthy kind of fellows,
So low, one wonders they were not born dogs,
Can do as well, alas!
    ADALMAR   There's cunning in thee.
A year ago this doctrine might have pleased me:
But since, I have remembered in my childhood   145
My teachers told me that I was immortal,
And had within me something like a god;
Now, by believing firmly in that promise,
I do enjoy a part of its fulfilment,
And, antedating my eternity,   150
Act as I were immortal.
    DUKE   Think of *now*.
This Hope and Memory are wild horses, tearing
The precious *now* to pieces. Grasp and use
The breath within you; for you know not, whether
That wind about the trees brings you one more.   155
Thus far yourself. But tell me, hath no other
A right, which you would injure? Is this sceptre,
Which you would stamp to dust and let each varlet
Pick out his grain of power; this great spirit,
This store of mighty men's concentrate souls,   160
Which kept your fathers in gods' breath, and you
Would waste in the wide, smoky, pestilent air
For every dog to snuff in; is this royalty
Your own? O! when you were a boy, young prince,
I would have laid my heart upon your spirit: 165
Now both are broken.
    ADALMAR   Father?
    DUKE   Yes, my son:
We'll live to be most proud of those two names.
Go on thy way: I follow and o'erlook.
This pilgrim's shape will hang about and guard thee,
Being but the shadow of my sunniness,   170
Looking in patience through a cloudy time.   [*Exeunt.*

SCENE II. *A garden*

SIBYLLA *and* ATHULF

ATHULF From me no comfort. O you specious creatures,
So poisonous to the eye! Go! you sow madness:
And one of you, although I cannot curse her,
Will make my grave a murderer's. I'll do nought;
But rather drink and revel at your bridal. 5
And why not Isbrand? Many such a serpent
Doth lick heaven's dew out of as sweet a flower.
Wed, wed! I'll not prevent it.
SIBYLLA   I beseech thee,
If there be any tie of love between thee
And she who is thy brother's.
ATHULF   Curse the word! 10
And trebly curse the deed that made us brothers!
O that I had been born the man I hate!
Any, at least, but one. Then — sleep my soul;
And walk not in thy sleep to do the act,
Which thou must ever dream of. My fair lady, 15
I would not be the reason of one tear
Upon thy bosom, if the times were other;
If women were not women. When the world
Goes round the other way, and doing Cain-like
Passes as merrily as doing Eve-like, 20
Then I'll be pitiful. Let go my hand;
It is a mischievous limb, and may run wild,
Doing the thing its master would not.
Lo! Here comes some holy father to console you.   [*Exit.*
SIBYLLA Then no one hears me. O! the world's too loud, 25
With trade and battle, for my feeble cry
To rouse the living. The invisible
Hears best what is unspoken; and my thoughts
Have long been calling comfort from the grave.
                    Enter WOLFRAM
WOLFRAM Lady, you called me.
SIBYLLA   I?
WOLFRAM   The word was *Comfort*: 30
A name by which the master, whose I am,
Is named by many wise and many wretched.
Will ye with me to the place where sighs are not;

A shore of blessing, which disease doth beat
Sea-like, and dashes those whom he would wreck   35
Into the arms of Peace? But ah! what say I?
You're young and must be merry in the world;
Have friends to envy, lovers to betray you;
And feed young children with the blood of your heart,
Till they have sucked up strength enough to break it.   40
Poor woman! Art thou nothing but the straw
Bearing a heavy poison, and, that shed,
Cut down to be stamped on? But thou'rt i' th' blade,
The green and milky sun-deceived grass:
So stand till the scythe comes, take shine and shower,   45
And the wind fell you gently.
    SIBYLLA   Do not go.
Speak as at first you did; there was in the words
A mystery and music, which did thaw
The hard old rocky world into a flood,
Whereon a swan-drawn boat seemed at my feet   50
Rocking on its blue billows; and I heard
Harmonies, and breathed odours from an isle,
Whose flowers cast tremulous shadows in the day
Of an immortal sun, and crowd the banks
Whereon immortal human kind doth couch.   55
This I have dreamt before: your speech recalled it.
So speak to soothe me once again.
    WOLFRAM (*Aside*)   Snake Death,
Sweet as the cowslip's honey is thy whisper:
O let this dove escape thee! I'll not plead,
I will not be thy suitor to this innocent: 60
Open thy craggy jaws; speak, coffin-tongued,
Persuasions through the dancing of the yew-bough
And the crow's nest upon it. (*Aloud*) Lady fair,
Listen not to me, look not on me more.
I have a fascination in my words,   65
A magnet in my look, which drags you downwards,
From hope and life. You set your eyes upon me,
And think I stand upon this earth beside you:
Alas! I am upon a jutting stone,
Which crumbles down the steeps of an abyss;   70
And you, above me far, grow wild and giddy:
Leave me, or you must fall into the deep.

SIBYLLA I leave thee never, nor thou me. O no!
You know not what a heart you spurn away;
How good it might be, if love cherished it;   75
And how deserted 'tis; ah, so deserted,
That I have often wished a ghost would come,
Whose love might haunt it. Turn not thou, the last.
Thou see'st I'm young: how happy might I be!
And yet I only wish these tears I shed   80
Were raining on my grave. If thou'lt not love me,
Then do me the next office; show me only
The shortest path to solitary death.
    WOLFRAM You're moved to wildness, maiden. Beg not of me.
I can grant nothing good: quiet thyself,   85
And seek heaven's help. Farewell.
    SIBYLLA   Wilt thou leave me?
Unpitying, aye unmoved in cheek and heart,
Stern, selfish mortal? Hast thou heard my prayer;
Hast seen me weep; hast seen my limbs to quiver,
Like a storm-shaken tree over its roots?   90
Art thou alive, and canst thou see this wretch,
Without a care?
    WOLFRAM   Thou see'st I am unmoved:
Infer the truth.
    SIBYLLA   Thy soul indeed is dead.
    WOLFRAM My soul, my soul! O that it wore not now
The semblance of a garb it hath cast off;   95
O that it was disrobed of these mock limbs,
Shed by a rocky birth unnaturally,
Long after their decease and burial!
O woe that I must speak! for she, who hears,
Is marked for no more breathing. There are histories   100
Of women, nature's bounties, who disdained
The mortal love of the embodied man,
And sought the solitude which spirits cast
Around their darksome presence. These have loved,
Wooed, wedded, and brought home their moonstruck brides 105
Unto the world-sanded eternity.
Hast faith in such reports?
    SIBYLLA   So lonely am I,
That I dare wish to prove them true.
    WOLFRAM   Dar'st die?

A grave-deep question. Answer it religiously.
    SIBYLLA With him I loved, I dared.
    WOLFRAM   With me and for me.   110
I am a ghost. Tremble not; fear not me.
The dead are ever good and innocent,
And love the living. They are cheerful creatures,
And quiet as the sunbeams, and most like,
In grace and patient love and spotless beauty,   115
The new-born of mankind. 'Tis better too
To die, as thou art, young, in the first grace
And full of beauty, and so be remembered
As one chosen from the earth to be an angel;
Not left to droop and wither, and be borne   120
Down by the breath of time. Come then, Sibylla,
For I am Wolfram!
    SIBYLLA   Thou art come to fetch me!
It is indeed a proof of boundless love,
That thou hadst need of me even in thy bliss.
I go with thee. O Death! I am thy friend,   125
I struggle not with thee, I love thy state:
Thou canst be sweet and gentle, be so now;
And let me pass praying away into thee,
As twilight still does into starry night.   [*Exeunt.*

SCENE III. *A garden, under the windows of* AMALA'*s apartment*

ATHULF
  ATHULF Once more I'll see thee, love, speak to thee, hear thee;
And then my soul shall cut itself a door
Out of this planet. I've been wild and heartless,
Laughed at the feasts where Love had never place,
And pledged my light faith to a hundred women,   5
Forgotten all next day. A worthless life,
A life ridiculous! Day after day,
Folly on folly! But I'll not repent.
Remorse and weeping shall not be my virtues:
Let fools do both, and, having had their evil,   10
And tickled their young hearts with the sweet sins
That feather Cupid's shafts, turn timid, weep,
Be penitent. Now the wild banquet's o'er,

Wine spilt, lights out, I cannot brook the world,
It is so silent. And that poisonous reptile, 15
My past self, is a villain I'll not pardon.
I hate and will have vengeance on my soul:
Satirical Murder, help me … Ha! I am
Devil-inspired: out with you, ye fool's thoughts!
You're young, strong, healthy yet; years may you live: 20
Why yield to an ill-humoured moment? No!
I'll cut his throat across, make her my wife;
Huzza! for a mad life! and be a Duke!
I was born for sin and love it.
                      O thou villain,
Die, die! Have patience with me, heavenly Mercy! 25
Let me but once more look upon that blessing,
Then can I calmly offer up to thee
This crime-haired head.
            Enter AMALA *as bride, with a bridesmaid*
                O beauty, beauty!
Thou shed'st a moony night of quiet through me.
Thanks! now I am resolved.
   BRIDESMAID   Amala, good night: 30
Thou'rt happy. In these high delightful times,
It does the human heart much good to think
On deepest woe, which may be waiting for us,
Masked even in a marriage-hour.
   AMALA   Thou'rt timid:
'Tis well to trust in a good genius. 35
Are not our hearts, in these great pleasures godded,
Let out awhile to their eternity
And made prophetic? The past is pale to me;
But I do see my future plain of life,
Full of rejoicings and of harvest-dances, 40
Clearly, it is so sunny. A year hence
I'll laugh at you for this, until you weep.
Good night, sweet fear.
   BRIDESMAID   Take this flower from me,
(A white rose, fitting for a wedding-gift,)
And lay it on your pillow. Pray to live 45
So fair and innocently; pray to die,
Leaf after leaf, so softly.   *[Exit.*
   AMALA — Now to my chamber; yet an hour or two,

In which years must be sown.
    ATHULF   Stay, Amala;
An old acquaintance brings a greeting to you,   50
Upon your wedding night.
    AMALA His brother Athulf! What can he do here?
I fear the man.
    ATHULF   Dost love him?
    AMALA   That were cause
Indeed to fear him. Leave me, leave me, sir;
It is too late. We cannot be together   55
For any good.
    ATHULF   This once we can. O Amala,
Had I been in my young days taught the truth,
And brought up with the kindness and affection
Of a good man! I was not myself evil,
But out of youth and ignorance did much wrong.   60
Had I received lessons in thought and nature,
We might have been together, but not thus.
How then? Did you not love me long ago?
More, O much more than him? Yes, Amala,
You would have been mine now. A life with thee,   65
Heavenly delight and virtue ever with us!
I've lost it, trod on it, and spurned it. Woe!
O bitter woe is me!
    AMALA   Athulf, why make me
Rue the inevitable? Prithee leave me.
    ATHULF Thee bye and bye: and all that is not thee.   70
Thee, my all, that I've forfeited I'll leave,
And the world's all, my nothing.
    AMALA   Nay; despond not.
Thou'lt be a merry, happy man some day,
And list to this as to a tale of some one
You had forgotten.
    ATHULF   Now no need of comfort: 75
I'm somehow glad that it did thus fall out.
Then had I lived too softly; in these woes
I can stand up, and show myself a man.
I do not think that I shall live an hour.
Wilt pardon me for that my earlier deeds   80
Have caused to thee of sorrow? Amala,
Pity me, pardon me, bless me in this hour;

In this my death, in this your bridal, hour.
Pity me, sweet.
  AMALA Both thee and me: no more!
  ATHULF   Forgive!
  AMALA With all my soul. God bless thee, my dear Athulf. 85
  ATHULF Kiss I thy hand? O much more fervently
Now, in my grief, than heretofore in love.
Farewell, go; look not back again upon me.
In silence go.   [*Exit* AMALA.
     She having left my eyes,
There's nothing in the world, to look on which 90
I'd live a moment longer. Therefore come,
Thou sacrament of death: Eternity,
I pledge thee thus.   [*He drinks from a vial.*
     How cold and sweet! It seems
As if the earth already began shaking,
To sink beneath me. O ye dead, come near; 95
Why see I you not yet? Come, crowd about me;
Under the arch of this triumphal hour,
Welcome me; I am one of you, and one
That, out of love for you, have forced the doors
Of the stale world.   100
     Enter ADALMAR
  ADALMAR I'm wearied to the core: where's Amala?
Ha! Near her chambers! Who?
  ATHULF   Ask that to-morrow
Of the marble, Adalmar. Come hither to me.
We must be friends: I'm dying.
  ADALMAR   How?
  ATHULF   The cup,
I've drank myself immortal.
  ADALMAR   You are poisoned? 105
  ATHULF I am blessed, Adalmar. I've done't myself.
'Tis nearly passed, for I begin to hear
Strange but sweet sounds, and the loud rocky dashing
Of waves, where time into Eternity
Falls over ruined worlds. The wind is fair, 110
The boat is in the bay,
And the fair mermaid pilot calls away.
  ADALMAR Self poisoned?
  ATHULF   Aye: a philosophic deed.

Go and be happy.
    ADALMAR   God! What hast thou done?
    ATHULF Justice upon myself.
    ADALMAR   No. Thou hast stolen   115
The right of the deserving good old man
To rest, his cheerful labour being done.
Thou hast been wicked; caused much misery;
Dishonoured maidens; broken fathers' hearts;
Maddened some; made others wicked as thyself;   120
And darest thou die, leaving a world behind thee
That groans of thee to heaven?
    ATHULF   If I thought so —
Terrible would it be: then I've both killed
And damned myself. There's justice!
    ADALMAR   Thou should'st have lived;
Devoting every minute to the work   125
Of useful, penitent amendment: then,
After long years, you might have knelt to Fate,
And ta'en her blow not fearing. Wretch, thou diest not,
But goest living into hell.
    ATHULF   It is too true;
I am deserted by those turbulent joys.   130
The fiend hath made me death-drunk. Here I'll lie,
And die most wretchedly, accursed, unpitied
Of all, most hated by myself. O God,
If thou could'st but repeal this fatal hour,
And let me live, how day and night I'd toil   135
For all things to atone! Must I wish vainly?
My brother, is there any way to live?
    ADALMAR For thee, alas! in this world there is none.
Think not upon't.
    ATHULF   Thou liest: there must be:
Thou know'st it, and dost keep it secret from me,   140
Letting me die for hate and jealousy.
O that I had not been so pious a fool,
But killed thee, 'stead of me, and had thy wife!
I should be at the banquet, drinking to her,
Kissing her lip, in her eye smiling…
                              Peace!   145
Thou see'st I'm growing mad: now leave me here,
Accursed as I am, alone to die.

O birth, O breath, O life!
   ADALMAR Wretched, yet not despised, farewell my brother.
   ATHULF O Arab, Arab! Thou dost sell true drugs.   150
Brother, my soul is very weary now:
Speak comfortably to me.
   ADALMAR   From the Arab,
From Ziba, had'st the poison?
   ATHULF   Aye. 'Twas good:
An honest villain is he.
   ADALMAR   Hold, sweet brother,
A little longer hold in hope on life;   155
But a few minutes more. I seek the sorcerer,
And he shall cure thee with some wondrous drug.
He can, and shall perform it: rest thee quiet:
Hope or revenge I'll bring thee.   [*Exit.*
   ATHULF   Dare I hope?
O no: methinks it is not so unlovely,   160
This calm unconscious state, this breathless peace,
Which all, but troublesome and riotous man,
Assume without resistance. Here I'll lay me,
And let life fall from off me tranquilly.
    Enter singers and musicians, led by SIEGFRIED; *they sing under*
                AMALA'S *windows*

Song
By female voices
We have bathed, where none have seen us,   165
  In the lake and in the fountain,
    Underneath the charmed statue
Of the timid, bending Venus,
  When the water-nymphs were counting
In the waves the stars of night,   170
    And those maidens started at you,
Your limbs shone through so soft and bright.
    But no secrets dare we tell,
      For thy slaves unlace thee,
      And he, who shall embrace thee,   175
    Waits to try thy beauty's spell.

By male voices
We have crowned thee queen of women,

Since love's love, the rose, hath kept her
Court within thy lips and blushes,
And thine eye, in beauty swimming, 180
Kissing, we rendered up the sceptre,
At whose touch the startled soul
Like an ocean bounds and gushes,
And spirits bend at thy controul.
But no secrets dare we tell, 185
For thy slaves unlace thee,
And he, who shall embrace thee,
Is at hand, and so farewell.

ATHULF Shame on you! Do you sing their bridal song
Ere I have closed mine eyes? Who's there among you 190
That dare to be enamoured of a maid
So far above you, ye poor rhyming knaves?
Ha! there begins another.

Song by SIEGFRIED
Maiden, thou sittest alone above,
Crowned with flowers and like a sprite 195
Starrily clothed in a garment white:
Thou art the only maiden I love,
And a soul of fondness to thee I bring,
Thy glorious beauty homaging, —
But ah! thou wearest a golden ring. 200

Maiden, thou'st broken no vow to me
But undone me alone with gentleness,
Wasting upon me glances that bless:
And knew'st that I never was born for thee.
No hope, no joy, yet never more 205
My heart shall murmur; now 'tis o'er,
I'll bless thee, dying at thy door.

ATHULF Ha! Ha! That fellow moves my spleen;
A disappointed and contented lover.
Methinks he's above fifty by his voice: 210
If not, he should be whipped about the town,
For vending such tame doctrine in love-verses.
Up to the window, carry off the bride,

And away on horseback, squeaker!
   SIEGFRIED Peace, thou bold drunken fellow that liest
                                   there! — 215
Leave him to sleep his folly out, good fellows.
                   [*Exit with the musicians, &c.*
   ATHULF Well said: I do deserve it. I lie here
A thousand-fold fool, dying ridiculously
Because I could not have the girl I fancied.
Well, thy are wedded; how long now will last   220
Affection or content? Besides 'twere possible
He might have quaffed a like draught. But 'tis done:
Villainous idiot that I am to think on't.
She willed it so. Then, Amala, be fearless:
Wait but a little longer in thy chamber,   225
And he will be with thee whom thou hast chosen:
Or, if it make thee pastime, listen sweet one,
And I will sing to thee, here in the moonlight,
Thy bridal song and my own dirge in one.

                     Song
   A cypress-bough, and a rose-wreath sweet,   230
   A wedding-robe, and a winding-sheet,
     A bridal-bed and a bier.
   Thine be the kisses, maid,
     And smiling Love's alarms;
   And thou, pale youth, be laid   235
     In the grave's cold arms.
   Each in his own charms,
     Death and Hymen both are here;
      So up with scythe and torch,
      And to the old church porch,   240
     While all the bells ring clear:
   And rosy, rosy the bed shall bloom,
   And earthy, earthy heap up the tomb.

   Now tremble dimples on your cheek,
   Sweet be your lips to taste and speak,   245
     For he who kisses is near:
   For her the bridegroom fair,
     In youthful power and force;
   For him the grizard bare,

Pale knight on a pale horse,   250
To woo him to a corpse.
  Death and Hymen both are here;
    So up with scythe and torch,
    And to the old church porch,
  While all the bells ring clear: 255
And rosy, rosy the bed shall bloom,
And earthy, earthy heap up the tomb.

ATHULF Now we'll lie down and wait for our two summoners;
Each patiently at least.
                        Enter AMALA
                  O thou kind girl,
Art thou again there? Come and lay thine hand   260
In mine; and speak again thy soft way to me.
    AMALA Thy voice is fainter, Athulf: why sang'st thou?
    ATHULF It was my farewell: now I'll sing no more;
Nor speak a great deal after this. 'Tis well
You weep not. If you had esteemed me much,   265
It were a horrible mistake of mine.
Wilt close my eyes when I am dead, sweet maid?
    AMALA O Athulf, thou might'st still have lived.
    ATHULF   What boots it,
And thou not mine, not even loving me?
But that makes dying very sad to me.   270
Yet even thy pity is worth much.
    AMALA   O no;
I pity not alone, but I am wretched —
Love thee and ever did most fervently,
Still hoping thou would'st turn and merit it.
But now — O God! if life were possible to thee,   275
I'd be thy friend for ever.
    ATHULF O thou art full of blessings!
Thou lovest me, Amala: one kiss, but one;
It is not much to grant a dying man.
    AMALA I am thy brother's bride, forget not that;   280
And never but to this, thy dying ear,
Had I confessed so much in such an hour.
But this be too forgiven. Now farewell.
'Twere not amiss if I should die to-night:
Athulf, my love, my only love, farewell.   285

ATHULF Yet one more minute. If we meet hereafter,
Wilt thou be mine? I have the right to thee;
And, if thou promise, I will let him live
This life, unenvied, with thee.
   AMALA   Athulf, I will:
Our bliss there will be greater for the sorrow   290
We now in parting feel.
   ATHULF   I go, to wait thee. [*Exit* AMALA.
Farewell, my bliss! She loves me with her soul,
And I might have enjoyed her, were he fallen.
Ha! ha! and I am dying like a rat,
And he shall drink his wine, twenty years hence,   295
Beside his cherished wife, and speak of me
With a compassionate smile! Come, Madness, come,
For death is loitering still.
       Enter ADALMAR *and* ZIBA
   ADALMAR   An antidote!
Restore him whom thy poisons have laid low,
If thou wilt not sup with thy fellow fiends   300
In hell to-night.
   ZIBA   I pray thee strike me not.
It was his choice; and why should he be breathing
Against his will?
   ATHULF   Ziba, I need not perish.
Now my intents are changed: so, if thou canst,
Dispense me life again.
   ADALMAR   Listen to him,   305
And once be a preserver.
   ZIBA   Let him rise.
Why, think you that I'd deal a benefit,
So precious to the noble as is death,
To such a pampered darling of delight
As he that shivers there? O, not for him,   310
Blooms my dark Nightshade, nor doth Hemlock brew
Murder for cups within her cavernous root.
Not for him is the metal blessed to kill,
Nor lets the poppy her leaves fall for him.
To heroes such are sacred. He may live,   315
As long as 'tis the Gout and Dropsy's pleasure.
He wished to play at suicide, and swallowed
A draught, that may depress and shake his powers

Until he sleeps awhile; then all is o'er.
And so good night, my princes.   [*Exit.*
    ADALMAR   Dost thou hear?   320
    ATHULF Victory! victory! I *do* hear; and Fate hears,
And plays with Life for one of our two souls,
With dice made of death's bones. But shall I do't?
O Heaven! it is a fearful thing to be so saved!
    ADALMAR Now, brother, thou'lt be happy.
    ATHULF   With thy wife!   325
I tell thee, hapless brother, on my soul,
Now that I live, I *will* live; I alone;
And Amala alone shall be my love.
There's no more room for you, since you have chosen
The woman and the power which I covet.   330
Out of thy bridal bed, out of thy throne!
Away to Abel's grave.   [*Stabs* ADALMAR.
    ADALMAR   Thou murderous traitor!
I was thy brother.   [*Dies.*
    ATHULF (*After a pause*) How long a time it is since I was here!
And yet I know not whether I have slept,   335
Or wandered through a dreary cavernous forest,
Struggling with monsters. 'Tis a quiet place,
And one inviting strangely to deep rest.
I have forgotten something; my whole life
Seems to have vanished from me to this hour.   340
There was a foe whom I should guard against;
Who is he?
    AMALA (*From her window*) Adalmar!
    ATHULF (*In a low voice*) Hush! hush! I come to thee.
Let me but see if he be dead: speak gently,
His jealous ghost still hears.
    AMALA   So, it is over
With that poor troubled heart! O then to-night   345
Leave me alone to weep.
    ATHULF   As thou wilt, lady.
I'm stunned with what has happened. He is dead.
    AMALA O night of sorrow! Bear him from the threshold.
None of my servants must know where and why
He sought his grave. Remove him. O poor Athulf,   350
Why did'st thou it? I'll to my bed and mourn.   [*Retires.*
    ATHULF Hear'st thou, corpse, how I play thy part? Thus had he

Pitied me in fraternal charity,
And I lain there so helpless. But what's this?
That chills my blood and darkens so my eyes?   355
What's going on in my heart and in my brain,
My bones, my life, all over me, all through me?
It cannot last. No longer shall I be
What I am now. Oh! I am changing, changing,
Dreadfully changing! Even here and now   360
A transformation will o'ertake and seize me.
It is God's sentence whispered over me.
I am unsouled, dishumanized, uncreated;
My passions swell and grow like human beasts conceived;
My feet are fixing roots, and every limb   365
Is billowy and gigantic, till I seem
A wild old wicked mountain in the sea:
And the abhorred conscience of this murder,
Shall be created and become a Lion
All alone in the darkness of my spirit,   370
And lair him in my caves,
And when I lie tremendous in the billows,
Murderers, and men half ghosts, stricken with madness,
Will come to live upon my rugged sides,
Die, and be buried in it. Now it comes;   375
I break, and magnify, and lose my form.
And yet I shall be taken for a man,
And never be discovered till I die.
Terrible, terrible: damned before my time,
In secret! 'Tis a dread, o'erpowering phantom.   380
                  [*He lies down by the body, and sleeps: the scene closes.*

SCENE IV. *A large hall in the ducal castle. Through the windows in
the background appears the illuminated city.*

Enter ISBRAND *and* SIEGFRIED
ISBRAND By my grave, Siegfried, 'tis a wedding-night.
The wish, that I have courted from my boyhood,
Comes blooming, crowned, to my embrace. Methinks,
The spirit of the city is right lovely;
And she will leave her rocky body sleeping   5
To-night, to be my queenly paramour.

Has it gone twelve?
    SIEGFRIED   This half hour. Here I've set
A little clock, that you may mark the time.
    ISBRAND Its hand divides the hour. Are our guards here,
About the castle?
    SIEGFRIED   You've a thousand swordsmen,   10
Strong and true soldiers, at the stroke of one.
    ISBRAND One's a good hour; a ghostly hour. To-night
The ghost of a dead planet shall walk through,
And shake the pillars of this dukedom down.
The princes both are occupied and lodged   15
Far from us: that is well; they will hear little.
Go once more round, to the towers and battlements:
The hour, that strikes, says to our hearts 'Be one';
And, with one motion of a hundred arms,
Be the beacons fired, the alarums rung,   20
And tyrants slain! Be busy.
    SIEGFRIED   I am with them.   [*Exit.*
    ISBRAND Mine is the hour it strikes; my first of life.
To morrow, with what pity and contempt,
Shall I look back new-born upon myself!
               Enter a servant
                  What now?
    SERVANT The banquet's ready.
    ISBRAND   Let it wait awhile: 25
The wedding is not ended. That shall be
No common banquet: none sit there, but souls
That have outlived a lower state of being.
Summon the guests.   [*Exit servant.*
            Some shall have bitter cups,
The honest shall be banished from the board   30
And the knaves duped by a luxurious bait.
    Enter the DUKE, TORWALD, *and other guests and conspirators*
Friends, welcome hither in the prince's name,
Who has appointed me his deputy
To-night. Why this is right: while men are here,
They should keep close and warm and thick together,   35
Many abreast. Our middle life is broad;
But life and death, the turnstiles that admit us
On earth and off it, send us, one by one,
A solitary walk. Lord governor,

Will you not sit?
    TORWALD   You are a thrifty liver,   40
Keeping the measure of your time beside you.
    ISBRAND Sir, I'm a melancholy, lonely man,
A kind of hermit: and to meditate
Is all my being. One has said, that time
Is a great river running to eternity.   45
Methinks 'tis all one water, and the fragments,
That crumble off our ever-dwindling life,
Dropping into't, first make the twelve-houred circle,
And that spreads outwards to the great round Ever.
    TORWALD You're fanciful.
    ISBRAND   A very ballad-maker.   50
We quiet men must think and dream at least.
Who likes a rhyme among us? My lord governor,
'Tis tedious waiting until supper time:
Shall I read some of my new poetry?
One piece at least?
    TORWALD   Well; without further preface,   55
If it be brief.
    ISBRAND   A fragment, quite unfinished,
Of a new ballad called 'The Median Supper'.
It is about Astyages; and I
Differ in somewhat from Herodotus.
But altering the facts of history,   60
When they are troublesome, good governors
Will hardly visit rigorously. Attention!

      'Harpagus, hast thou salt enough,
        Hast thou broth enough to thy kid?
      And hath the cook put right good stuff   65
        Under the pasty lid?'

      'I've salt enough, Astyages,
        And broth enough in sooth;
      And the cook hath mixed the meat and grease
        Most tickling to my tooth.'   70

      So spake no wild Red Indian swine,
        Eating a forest rattle-snake:
      But Harpagus, that Mede of mine,

And King Astyages so spake.

'Wilt have some fruit? Wilt have some wine?   75
    Here's what is soft to chew;
I plucked it from a tree divine,
    More precious never grew.'

Harpagus took the basket up,
    Harpagus brushed the leaves away;   80
But first he filled a brimming cup,
    For his heart was light and gay.

And then he looked, and saw a face,
    Chopped from the shoulders of some one;
And who alone could smile in grace   85
    So sweet? Why, Harpagus, thy son.

'Alas!' quoth the king, 'I've no fork,
    Alas! I've no spoon of relief,
Alas! I've no neck of a stork
    To push down this throttling grief.   90

We've played at kid for child, lost both;
    I'd give you the limbs if I could;
Some lie in your platter of broth:
    Good night, and digestion be good.'

Now Harpagus said not a word,   95
    Did no eye-water spill:
His heart replied, for that had heard;
    And hearts' replies are still.

How do you like it?
        DUKE   Poetry, they say,
Should be the poet's soul; and here, methinks,   100
In every word speaks yours.
        ISBRAND   Good. Don't be glad too soon.
Do ye think I've done? Three minutes' patience more.

    A cannibal of his own boy,
        He is a cannibal uncommon;

And Harpagus, he is my joy, 105
   Because he wept not like a woman.

From the old supper-giver's poll
   He tore the many-kingdomed mitre;
To him, who cost him his son's soul,
   He gave it; to the Persian fighter: 110
         And quoth,
'Old art thou, but a fool in blood:
   If thou hast made me eat my son,
Cyrus hath ta'en his grandsire's food;
   There's kid for child, and who has won? 115

All kingdomless is thy old head,
   In which began the tyrannous fun;
Thou'rt slave to him, who should be dead:
   There's kid for child, and who has won?'

Now let the clock strike, let the clock strike now, 120
And world be altered!
  [*The clock strikes one, and the hour is repeated from the steeples of the*
                                                  city.
                     Trusty timepiece,
Thou hast struck a mighty hour, and thy work's done;
For never shalt thou count a meaner one.
                       [*He dashes it on the ground.*
Thus let us break our old life of dull hours,
And hence begin a being, counted not 125
By minutes, but by glories and delights.
                [*Steps to a window and throws it open.*
Thou steepled city, that dost lie below,
Time doth demand whether thou wilt be free.
Now give thine answer.
  [*A trumpet is heard, followed by a peal of cannon. Beacons are seen.*
                      The stage is lined with soldiery.
  TORWALD   Traitor, desperate traitor!
Yet betrayed traitor! Make a path for me, 130
Or, by the majesty that thou offendest,
Thou shalt be struck with lightning in thy triumph.
  ISBRAND   *All kingdomless is the old mule,*
          In which began the tyrannous fun;

> *Thou'rt slave to him, who was thy fool;*   135
> *There's Duke for Brother; who has won?*

Take the old man away.

TORWALD   I go: but my revenge

Hangs, in its unseen might, godlike around you.   [*Exit guarded.*

ISBRAND To work, my friends, to work! Each man his way.

These present instants, cling to them: hold fast;   140

And spring from this one to the next; still upwards.

They're rungs to Jacob's ladder to scale heaven with:

Haste, or 'tis drawn away.   [*Exeunt cæteri.*

                    O stingy nature,

To make me but one man! Had I but body

For every several measure of thought and will,   145

This night should see me world-crowned.

                    Enter a messenger

                    What news bring'st thou?

MESSENGER Friends of the governor hold the strongest tower,

And shoot with death's own arrows.

ISBRAND   Get thee back,

And never let me hear thy voice again,

Unless to say, ''Tis taken'. Hark ye, sirrah;   150

Wood in its walls, lead on its roof, the tower

Cries, 'Burn me!' Go and cut away the drawbridge,

And leave the quiet fire to himself:

He knows his business.   [*Exit messenger.*

                    Enter ZIBA *armed*

                    What with you?

ZIBA   I'll answer,

When one of us is undermost.

ISBRAND   Ha! Midnight,   155

Can a slave fight?   [*They fight:* ZIBA *is disarmed.*

                    Now darest thou cry for mercy?

ZIBA Never. Eternity! Come give me that,

And I will thank thee.

ISBRAND   Something like man,

And something like a fool. Thou'rt such a reptile,

That I do like thee: pick up thy black life: 160

I would not make my brother King and Fool,

Friend Death, so poor a present. Hence!   [*Exit* ZIBA.

                    They're busy.

'Tis a hot hour, which Murder steals from Love,

To create ghosts in.

Enter SIEGFRIED

Now?

SIEGFRIED Triumph! They cannot stand another half hour. 165
The loyal had all supped and gone to bed:
When our alarums thundered, they could only
Gaze from their frighted windows: and some few
We had in towers and churches to besiege.
But, when one hornet's nest was burnt, the rest   170
Cried quarter, and went home to end their naps.
ISBRAND 'Twas good. I knew it was well planned. Return,
And finish all. I'll follow thee, and see
How Mars looks in his night-cap.   [*Exit* SIEGFRIED.
O! it is nothing now to be a man.   175
Adam, thy soul was happy that it wore
The first, new, mortal members. To have felt
The joy of the first year, when the one spirit
Kept house-warming within its fresh-built clay,
I'd be content to be as old a ghost.   180
Thine was the hour to live in. Now we're common,
And man is tired of being no more than human;
And I'll be something better: — not by tearing
This chrysalis of psyche ere its hour,
Will I break through Elysium. There are sometimes,   185
Even here, the means of being more than men:
And I by wine, and women, and the sceptre,
Will be, my own way, heavenly in my clay.
O you small star-mob, had I been one of you,
I would have seized the sky some moonless night,   190
And made myself the sun; whose morrow rising
Shall see me new-created by myself.
Come, come; to rest, my soul. I must sleep off
This old plebeian creature that I am.   [*Exit.*

ACT V

SCENE I. *An apartment in the ducal castle*

ISBRAND *and* SIEGFRIED

SIEGFRIED They wait still for you in their council chamber,
And clamorously demand the keys of the treasure,
The stores of arms, lists of the troops you've hired,
Reports of your past acts, and your intentions
Towards the new republic.

ISBRAND   They demand!   5
A phrase politer would have pleased me more.
The puppets, whose heart-strings I hold and play
Between my thumb and fingers, this way, that way;
Through whose masks, wrinkled o'er by age and passion,
My voice and spirit hath spoken continually;   10
Dare now to ape free will? Well done, Prometheus!
Thou'st pitied Punch and given him a soul,
And all his wooden peers. The tools I've used
To chisel an old heap of stony laws,
The abandoned sepulchre of a dead dukedom,   15
Into the form my spirit loved and longed for;
Now that I've perfected her beauteous shape,
And animated it with half my ghost;
Now that I lead her to our bridal bed,
Dare the mean instruments to lay their plea,   20
Or their demand forsooth, between us? Go;
And tell the fools, (you'll find them pale, and dropping
Cold tears of fear out of their trembling cheek-pores;)
Tell them, for comfort, that I only laughed;
And bid them all to sup with me to-night,   25
When we will call the cup to counsel.

SIEGFRIED   Mean you
Openly to assume a kingly power,
Nor rather inch yourself into the throne?
Perhaps — but as you will.

ISBRAND   Siegfried, I'm one
That what I will must do, and what I do   30
Do in the nick of time without delay.
To-morrow is the greatest fool I know,
Excepting those that put their trust in him.

In one word hear, what soon they all shall hear:
A king's a man, and I will be no man   35
Unless I am a king. Why, where's the difference?
Throne steps divide us: they're soon climbed perhaps:
I have a bit of FIAT in my soul,
And can myself create my little world.
Had I been born a four-legged child, methinks   40
I might have found the steps from dog to man,
And crept into humanity. There be
Those that fall down out of their stage of manhood
Into the story where the four-legged dwell.
But to the conclave with my message quickly: 45
I've yet a deal to do.   [*Exit* SIEGFRIED.
        How I despise
All you mere men of muscle! It was ever
My study to find out a way to godhead,
And on reflection soon I found that first
I was but half created; that a power   50
Was wanting in my soul to be its soul,
And this was mine to make. Therefore I fashioned
A will above my will, that plays upon it,
As the first soul doth use in men and cattle.
There's lifeless matter; add the power of shaping,   55
And you've the crystal: add again the organs,
Wherewith to subdue sustenance to the form
And manner of oneself, and you've the plant:
Add power of motion, senses, and so forth,
And you've all kind of beasts; suppose a pig: 60
To pig add foresight, reason, and such stuff,
Then you have man. What shall we add to man,
To bring him higher? I begin to think
That's a discovery I soon shall make.
Thus I, owing nought to books, but being read   65
In the odd nature of much fish and fowl,
And cabbages and beasts, have I raised myself,
By this comparative philosophy,
Above your shoulders, my sage gentlemen.
Have patience but a little, and keep still,   70
I'll find means, bye and bye, of flying higher.   [*Exit.*

SCENE II. *Another apartment*

The DUKE, MARIO, ZIBA, *and Conspirators.* SIEGFRIED

A CONSPIRATOR (*to* SIEGFRIED) Said he nought else?

SIEGFRIED   What else he said was worse.
He is no more Isbrand of yesterday;
But looks and talks as one, who in the night
Hath made a bloody compact with some fiend.
His being is grown greater than it was,   5
And must make room, by cutting off men's lives,
For its shadowy increase.

CONSPIRATOR   O friends, what have we done?
Sold, for a promise, still security,
The mild familiar laws our fathers left;
Uprooted our firm country.

ZIBA   And now sit,   10
Weeping like babes, among its ruins. Up!
You have been cheated; now turn round upon him.
In this his triumph pull away his throne,
And let him into hell.

ANOTHER CONSPIRATOR But that I heard it
From you, his inmost counsel and next heart,   15
I'd not believe it. Why, the man was open;
We looked on him, and saw your looks reflected;
Your hopes and wishes found an echo in him;
He pleased us all, I think. Let's doubt the worst,
Until we see.

DUKE   Until you feel and perish.   20
You looked on him, and saw your looks reflected,
Because his soul was in a dark deep well,
And must draw down all others to encrease it:
Your hopes and wishes found an echo in him,
As out of a sepulchral cave, prepared   25
For you and them to sleep in. To be brief,
He is the foe of all; let all be his,
And he must be o'erwhelmed.

SIEGFRIED   I throw him off,
Although I feared to say so in his presence,
And think you all will fear. O that we had   30
Our good old noble Duke, to help us here!

DUKE Of him I have intelligence. The governor,

Whose guards are bribed and awed by these good tidings,
Waits us within. There we will speak at large:
And O! may justice, for this once, descend   35
Like lightning-footed vengeance.
    MARIO   It will come;
But when, I know not. Liberty, whose shade
Attends, smiles still in patience, and that smile
Melts tyrants down in time: and, till she bids,
To strike were unavailing.   [*Exeunt.* ZIBA *and* SIEGFRIED *remain.*
    ZIBA   Let them talk: 40
I mean to do; and will let no one's thoughts,
Or reasonable cooling counsels, mix
In my resolve to weaken it, as little
As shall a drop of rain or pity-water
Adulterate this thick blood-curdling liquor.   45
Siegfried, I'll free you from this thankless master.
    SIEGFRIED   I understand. To-night? Why that is best.
In plottings there is still some creak unstopped,
Some heart unsteeled, some fellow who doth talk
In sleep or in his cups, or tells his tale,   50
Love-drunk, unto his secret-selling mistress.
How shall't be done though?
    ZIBA   I'm his cup-bearer;
An office that he gave me in derision
And I will execute so cunningly
That he shall have no lips to laugh with, long;   55
Nor spare and spurn me, as he did last night.
Let him beware, who shows a dogged slave
Pity or mercy! For the drug, 'tis good:
There is a little, hairy, green-eyed snake,
Of voice like to the woody nightingale,   60
And ever singing pitifully sweet,
That nestles in the barry bones of death,
And is his dearest pet and playfellow.
The honied froth about that serpent's tongue
Deserves not so his habitation's name,   65
As doth this liquor. That's the liquor for him.   [*Exeunt.*

SCENE III. *A meadow*

SIBYLLA *and ladies, gathering flowers*

SIBYLLA Enough; the dew falls, and the glow-worm's shining:
Now let us search our baskets for the fairest
Among our flowery booty, and then sort them.

LADY The snowdrops are all gone; but here are cowslips,
And primroses, upon whose petals maidens,   5
Who love to find a moral in all things,
May read a lesson of pale bashfulness;
And violets, that have taught their young buds whiteness,
That blue-eyed ladies' lovers might not tear them
For the old comparison; daisies without number,   10
And buttercups and lilies of the vale.

SIBYLLA Sit then; and we will bind some up with rushes,
And wind us garlands. Thus it is with man;
He looks on nature as his supplement,
And still will find out likenesses and tokens   15
Of consanguinity, in the world's graces,
To his own being. So he loves the rose,
For the cheek's sake, whose touch is the most grateful
At night-fall to his lip; and, as the stars rise,
Welcomes the memories of delighting glances,   20
Which go up as an answer o'er his soul.

LADY And therefore earth and all its ornaments,
Which are the symbols of humanity
In forms refined, and efforts uncompleted,
All innocent and graceful, temper the heart,   25
Of him who muses and compares them skilfully,
To glad belief and tearful gratitude.
This is the sacred source of poesy.

SIBYLLA While we are young and free from care, we think so.
But, when old age or sorrow brings us nearer   30
To spirits and their interests, we see
Few features of mankind in outward nature;
But rather signs inviting us to heaven.
I love flowers too; not for a young girl's reason,
But because these brief visitors to us   35
Rise yearly from the neighbourhood of the dead,
To show us how far fairer and more lovely
Their world is; and return thither again,

Like parting friends that beckon us to follow,
And lead the way silent and smilingly. 40
Fair is the season when they come to us,
Unfolding the delights of that existence
Which is below us: 'tis the time of spirits,
Who with the flowers, and like them, leave their graves:
But when the earth is sealed, and none dare come 45
Upwards to cheer us, and man's left alone,
We have cold, cutting winter. For no bridal,
Excepting with the grave, are flowers fit emblems.
    LADY And why then do we pluck and wreathe them now?
    SIBYLLA Because a bridal with the grave is near. 50
You will have need of them to strew a corpse.
Aye, maidens, I am dying; but lament not:
It is to me a wished for change of being.
Yonder behold the evening star arising,
Appearing bright over the mountain-tops; 55
He has just died out of another region,
Perhaps a cloudy one; and so die I;
And the high heaven, serene and light with joy,
Which I pass into, will be my love's soul,
That will encompass me; and I shall tremble, 60
A brilliant star of never-dying delight,
'Mid the ethereal depth of his eternity.
Now lead me homewards: and I'll lay me down,
To sleep not, but to rest: then strew me o'er
With these flowers fresh out of the ghosts' abodes, 65
And they will lead me softly down to them. [*Exeunt.*

SCENE IV. *The ruined Cathedral, in which a large covered table with empty chairs is set; the sepulchre, and the cloisters painted with the* DANCE OF DEATH *as in Act III, Scene III. Moonlight. The clock strikes twelve; on which is heard*

A Song in the air
The moon doth mock and make me crazy,
    And midnight tolls her horrid claim
    On ghostly homage. Fie, for shame!
Deaths, to stand painted there so lazy.
There's nothing but the stars about us, 5
    And they're no tell-tales, but shine quiet:

Come out, and hold a midnight riot,
Where no mortal fool dare flout us:
And, as we rattle in the moonlight pale;
Wanderers shall think 'tis the nightingale.   10

[*The Deaths, and the figures paired with them, come out of the walls, and dance fantastically to a rattling music, singing; some seat themselves at the table and drink and with mocking gestures, mask the feast, &c.*

Song
Mummies and skeletons, out of your stones;
   Every age, every fashion, and figure of Death:
The death of the giant with petrified bones;
   The death of the infant who never drew breath.
Little and gristly, or bony and big,   15
   White and clattering, grassy and yellow;
The partners are waiting, so strike up a jig,
   Dance and be merry, for Death's a droll fellow.
The emperor and empress, the king and the queen,
   The knight and the abbot, friar fat, friar thin,   20
The gipsy and beggar, are met on the green;
   Where's Death and his sweetheart? We want to begin.
In circles, and mazes, and many a figure,
   Through clouds, over chimneys and cornfields yellow,
We'll dance and laugh at the red-nosed gravedigger,   25
   Who dreams not that Death is so merry a fellow.

One with a scythe, who has stood sentinel, now sings:
   Although my old ear
     Hath neither hammer nor drum,
   Methinks I can hear
     Living skeletons come.   30
The cloister re-echoes the call,
   And it frightens the lizard,
And, like an old hen, the wall
   Cries 'cluck! cluck! back to my gizzard;
    ''Tis warm, though it's stony,   35
    'My chickens so bony.'
So come let us hide, each with his bride,
For the wicked are coming who have not yet died.
        [*The Deaths return to their places in the wall.*

Enter ISBRAND, *the* DUKE, SIEGFRIED, MARIO, WOLFRAM *as fool, and
Conspirators, followed by* ZIBA *and other Attendants*

ISBRAND You wonder at my banqueting-house perhaps:
But 'tis my fashion, when the sky is clear,   40
To drink my wine out in the open air:
And this our sometime meeting-place is shadowy,
And the wind howleth through the ruins bravely.
Now sit, my gentle guests: and you, dark man,   [*To* WOLFRAM.
Make us as merry as you can, and proudly   45
Bear the new office, which your friend, the pilgrim,
Has begged for you: 'twas my profession once;
Do justice to that cap.
      DUKE Now, having washed our hearts of love and sorrow,
And pledged the rosiness of many a cheek,   50
And, with the name of many a lustrous maiden,
Ennobled enough cups; feed, once again,
Our hearing with another merry song.
      ISBRAND 'Tis pity that the music of this dukedom,
Under the former government, went wrong,   55
Like all the rest: my ministers shall look to't.
But sing again, my men.
      SIEGFRIED   What shall it be,
And of what turn? Shall battle's drum be heard?
The chase's trumpet? Shall the noise of Bacchus
Swell in our cheeks, or lazy, sorrowing love   60
Burthen with sighs our ballad?
      ISBRAND   Try the piece,
You sang me yesternight to sleep with best.
It is for such most profitable ends
We crowned folks encourage all the arts.

                    Song
    My goblet's golden lips are dry,   65
        And, as the rose doth pine
        For dew, so doth for wine
            My goblet's cup;
    Rain, O! rain, or it will die;
            Rain, fill it up!   70

    Arise, and get thee wings to-night,
        Ætna! and let run o'er

Thy wines, a hill no more,
　　But darkly frown
A cloud, where eagles dare not soar,　　　　　　　75
　　Dropping rain down.

ISBRAND　A very good and thirsty melody:
What say you to it, my court poet?
　WOLFRAM　Good melody! If this be a good melody,
I have at home, fattening in my stye,　　　　　　　80
A sow that grunts above the nightingale.
Why this will serve for those, who feed their veins
With crust, and cheese of dandelion's milk,
And the pure Rhine. When I am sick o' mornings,
With a horn-spoon tinkling my porridge-pot,　　　　85
'Tis a brave ballad: but in Bacchanal night,
O'er wine, red, black, or purple-bubbling wine,
That takes a man by the brain and whirls him round,
By Bacchus' lip! I like a full-voiced fellow,
A craggy-throated, fat-cheeked trumpeter,　　　　　90
A barker, a moon-howler, who could sing
Thus, as I heard the snaky mermaids sing
In Phlegethon, that hydrophobic river,
One May-morning in Hell.

　　　　　　　Song
Old Adam, the carrion crow,　　　　　　　　　　95
　　The old crow of Cairo;
He sat in the shower, and let it flow
　　Under his tail and over his crest;
　　　And through every feather
　　　Leaked the wet weather;　　　　　　　100
And the bough swung under his nest;
For his beak it was heavy with marrow.
　　Is that the wind dying? O no;
　　It's only two devils, that blow
　　Through a murderer's bones, to and fro,　　　105
　　　In the ghosts' moonshine.

Ho! Eve, my grey carrion wife,
　　When we have supped on kings' marrow,
Where shall we drink and make merry our life?

Our nest it is queen Cleopatra's scull,   110
    'Tis cloven and cracked,
    And battered and hacked,
But with tears of blue eyes it is full:
Let us drink then, my raven of Cairo.
    Is that the wind dying? O no;   115
    It's only two devils, that blow
    Through a murderer's bones, to and fro,
    In the ghosts' moonshine.

ISBRAND Pilgrim, it is with pleasure I acknowledge,
In this your friend, a man of genuine taste: 120
He imitates my style in prose and verse:
And be assured that this deserving man
Shall soon be knighted, when I have invented
The name of my new order; and perhaps
I'll make him minister. I pledge you, Fool: 125
Black! something exquisite.
    ZIBA   Here's wine of Egypt,
Found in a Memphian cellar, and perchance
Pressed from its fruit to wash Sesostris' throat,
Or sweeten the hot palate of Cambyses.
See how it pours, thick, clear, and odorous.   130
    ISBRAND 'Tis full, without a bubble on the top:
Pour him the like. Now give a toast.
    WOLFRAM   Excuse me:
I might offend perhaps, being blunt, a stranger,
And rustically speaking rustic thoughts.
    ISBRAND That shall not be: give us what toast you will,   135
We'll empty all our goblets at the word,
Without demur.
    SIEGFRIED   Well, since the stranger's silent,
I'll give a toast, which, I can warrant you,
Was yet ne'er drunk. There is a bony man,
Through whom the sun shines, when the sun is out: 140
Or the rain drops, when any clouds are weeping;
Or the wind blows, if Æolus will; his name,
And let us drink to his success and sanity; —
But will you truly?
    ISBRAND   Truly, as I said.
    SIEGFRIED Then round with the health of Death, round with

the health 145
Of Death the bony, Death the great; round, round.
Empty yourselves, all cups, unto the health
Of great King Death!
  WOLFRAM Set down the cup, Isbrand, set the cup down.
Drink not, I say.
   SIEGFRIED   And what's the matter now?   150
   ISBRAND What do you mean, by bidding me not drink?
Answer, I'm thirsty.
  WOLFRAM   Push aside the boughs:
Let's see the night, and let the night see us.
  ISBRAND Will the fool read us astronomic lectures?
  WOLFRAM Above stars; stars below; round the moon stars. 155
Isbrand, don't sip the grape-juice.
  ISBRAND   Must I drink,
Or not, according to a horoscope?
Says Jupiter, no? Then he's a hypocrite.
  WOLFRAM Look upwards, how 'tis thick and full, how sprinkled,
This heaven, with the planets. Now, consider;   160
Which will you have? The sun's already taken,
But you may find an oar in the half moon,
Or drive the comet's dragons; or, if you'd be
Rather a little snug and quiet god,
A one-horse star is standing ready for you.   165
Choose, and then drink.
  ISBRAND   If you are sane or sober,
What do you mean?
  WOLFRAM   It is a riddle, sir,
Siegfried, your friend, can solve.
  SIEGFRIED   Some sorry jest.
  WOLFRAM You'll laugh but palely at its sting, I think.
Hold the dog down; disarm him; grasp his right.   170
My lord, this worthy courtier loved your virtues
To such excess of piety, that he wished
To send you by a bye-path into heaven.
Drink, and you're straight a god — or something else.
  A CONSPIRATOR O murderous villain! Kill him where he
                  sits. 175
  ISBRAND Be quiet, and secure him. Siegfried, Siegfried;
Why hast thou no more genius in thy villainy?
Wilt thou catch kings in cobwebs? Lead him hence:

Chain him to-night in prison, and to-morrow
Put a cord round his neck and hang him up, 180
In the society of the old dog
Who killed my neighbour's sheep.
    SIEGFRIED   I do thank thee.
In faith, I hoped to have seen grass grow o'er you,
And should have much rejoiced. But, as it is,
I'll willingly die upright in the sun: 185
And I can better spare my life than you.
Good night then, Fool and Duke: you have my curse;
And Hell will have you some day down for hers:
So let us part like friends. My lords, good sleep
This night, the next I hope you'll be as well 190
As I shall. Should there be a lack of rope,
I recommend my bowstring as a strong one.
Once more, farewell: I wish you all, believe me,
Happily old, mad, sick, and dead, and cursed.   [*Exit guarded.*
    ISBRAND That gentleman should have applied his talent   195
To writing new-year's wishes. Another cup!
    WOLFRAM He has made us dull: so I'll begin a story.
As I was newly dead, and sat beside
My corpse, looking on it, as one who muses
Gazing upon a house he was burnt out of, 200
There came some merry children's ghosts to play
At hide-and-seek in my old body's corners: —
    ISBRAND But how came you to die and yet be here?
    WOLFRAM Did I say so? Excuse me. I am absent,
And forget always that I'm just now living. 205
But dead and living, which are which? A question
Not easy to be solved. Are you alone,
Men, as you're called, monopolists of life?
Or is all being, living? and *what is*,
With less of toil and trouble, more alive, 210
Than they, who cannot, half a day, exist
Without repairing their flesh mechanism?
Or do you owe your life, not to this body,
But to the sparks of spirit that fly off,
Each instant disengaged and hurrying 215
From little particles of flesh that die?
If so, perhaps you are the dead yourselves:
And these ridiculous figures on the wall

Laugh, in their safe existence, at the prejudice,
That you are anything like living beings.   220
But hark! The bell tolls, and a funeral comes.
                    [*Enter a funeral; ladies bearing a pall.*

                    Dirge
      We do lie beneath the grass
        In the moonlight, in the shade
      Of the yew-tree. They that pass
        Hear us not. We are afraid   225
          They would envy our delight,
          In our graves by glow-worm night.
      Come follow us, and smile as we;
          We sail to the rock in the ancient waves,
      Where the snow falls by thousands into the sea,   230
          And the drowned and the shipwrecked have happy graves.
                                    [*Exeunt.*

DUKE What's this that comes and goes, so shadow-like?
ATTENDANT They bear the fair Sibylla to her grave.
DUKE   She dead!
Darest thou do this, thou grave-begotten man,
Thou son of Death? (*To* WOLFRAM)
    WOLFRAM   Sibylla dead already?   235
I wondered how so fair a thing could live:
And, now she is no more, it seems to me
She was too beautiful ever to die!
    ISBRAND She, who was to have been my wife? Here, fellow;
Take thou this flower to strew upon her grave,   240
A lily of the valley; it bears bells,
For even the plants, it seems, must have their fool,
So universal is the spirit of folly;
And whisper, to the nettles of her grave,
'King Death hath asses' ears'.   245
    MARIO (*Stabbing* ISBRAND) At length thou art condemned to
                                    punishment.
Down, thou usurper, to the earth and grovel!
The pale form, that has led me up to thee,
Bids me deal this; and, now my task is o'er,
Beckons me hence.   [*Exit.*
    ISBRAND   Villain, thou dig'st deep: 250

But think you I will die? No: should I groan,
And close my eyes, be fearful of me still.
'Tis a good jest: I but pretend to die,
That you may speak about me bold and loudly;
Then I come back and punish: or I go   255
To dethrone Pluto. It is wine I spilt,
Not blood, that trickles down.
                    Enter TORWALD *with soldiers*
  TORWALD Long live duke Melveric!
  ALL Long live duke Melveric!
  ISBRAND   Duke Isbrand, long live he!
Duke Melveric is deposed.
  TORWALD   Receive the homage   260
Of your revolted city.
  DUKE   Torwald, thanks.
The usurper has his death-wound.
  TORWALD   Then cry, Victory!
And long life to duke Melveric! once more.
  ISBRAND I will live longer: when he's dead and buried,
A hundred years hence, or, it may be, more,   265
I shall return and take my dukedom back.
Imagine not I'm weak enough to die.
  WOLFRAM Meantime Death sends you back this cap of office.
At his court you're elected to the post:
Go, and enjoy it.   [*Sets the fool's cap on* ISBRAND'S *head.*
  ISBRAND   Bye and bye. But let not   270
Duke Melveric think that I part unrevenged:
For I hear in the clouds about me voices,
Singing
    All kingdomless is thy old head,
      In which began the tyrannous fun;   275
    He fetches thee, who should be dead;
      There's Duke for Brother! Who has won?
Now Death doth make indeed a fool of me.   [*Dies.*
  DUKE Where are my sons? I have not seen them lately.
Go to the bridegroom's lodgings, and to Athulf's,   280
And summon both.   [*Exit* ATTENDANT.
  WOLFRAM   They will be here; and sooner
Than you would wish. Meanwhile, my noble Duke,
Some friends of mine behind us seem to stir.
They wish, in honour of your restoration,

In memory also of your glorious deeds,   285
To present masque and dance to you. Is't granted?
  DUKE Surely; and they are welcome, for we need
Some merriment amid these sad events.
  WOLFRAM You in the wall there then, my thin light archers,
Come forth and dance a little: 'tis the season   290
When you may celebrate Death's Harvest-Home.
[*A dance of Deaths. In the middle of it enter* AMALA, *followed by a bier,*
    on which the corpse of ADALMAR *is borne. The dance goes out.*
  DUKE What's this? Another mummery?
  WOLFRAM   The antimasque,
I think they call it; 'tis satirical.
  AMALA My lord, you see the bridal bed that waits me.
Your son, my bridegroom, both no more, lies here,   295
Cold, pale, abandoned in his youthful blood:
And I his bride have now no duty further,
But to kneel down, wretched, beside his corpse,
Crying for justice on his murderers.
  DUKE Could my son die, and I not know it sooner?   300
Why, he is cold and stiff. O! now my crown
Is sunk down to the dust, my life is desolate.
Who did this deed?
                    Enter ATHULF
  WOLFRAM   Athulf, answer the call.
  AMALA O no! Suspect not him. He was last night
Gentle, and full of love, to both of us,   305
And could imagine ne'er so foul a deed.
Suspect not him; for so thou mak'st me feel
How terrible it is that he is dead,
Since his next friend's accused of such a murder:
And torture not his ghost, which must be here,   310
Striving in vain to utter one soul-sound,
To speak the guiltless free. Tempt not cruelly
The helplessness of him who is no more,
Nor make him discontented with the state,
Which lets him not assert his brother's innocence.   315
  DUKE (*To* ATHULF) Answer! Thou look'st like one, unto whose
                                                        soul
A secret voice, all day and night, doth whisper,
'Thou art a murderer'. Is it so? Then rather
Speak not. Thou wear'st a dagger at thy side;

Avenge the murdered man, thou art his brother;   320
And never let me hear from mortal lips
That my son was so guilty.
    ATHULF   Amala,
Still love me; weep some gentle drops for me;
And, when we meet again, fulfil thy promise.
Father, look here!   [*Stabs himself to death.* 325
    AMALA O Athulf! live one moment to deny it;
I ask that, and that only. Lo! old man,
He hath in indignation done the deed.
Since thou could'st think him for an instant guilty,
He held the life, which such a base suspicion   330
Had touched, and the old father who could speak it,
Unworthy of him more: and he did well.
I bade thee give me vengeance for my bridegroom,
And thou hast slain the only one who loved me.
Suspect and kill me too: but there's no need;   335
For such a one, as I, God never let
Live more than a few hours.   [*She falls into the arms of her ladies.*
    DUKE Torwald, the crown is yours; I reign no more.
But when, thou spectre, is thy vengeance o'er?
    WOLFRAM Melveric, all is finished, which to witness   340
The spirit of retribution called me hither.
Thy sons have perished for like cause, as that
For which thou did'st assassinate thy friend.
Sibylla is before us gone to rest.
Blessing and Peace to all who are departed!   345
But thee, who daredst to call up into life,
And the unholy world's forbidden sunlight,
Out of his grave him who reposed softly,
One of the ghosts doth summon, in like manner,
Thee, still alive, into the world o' th' dead.   350
                [*Exit with the* DUKE *into the sepulchre.*
             The curtain falls

Notes

The historical fact,* on which the preceding poem may be considered as founded, viz. that a Duke of Münsterberg in Silesia was stabbed to death by his court-fool, is to be found in Flögel's Gesch. d. Hofnarren Liegnitz v. Leipzig 1789. 8. S. 297 u. folg. A Silesian writer in Latin verse says

> Nam postquam Morio prolem
> forte lacessitus Bolconum extinxerat acri
> postremum jactu lateris (tum temporis aetas
> infaustum patriae ruiturae credidit omen)
> haeredem sterilit vt spes nulla resideret aulae.
>> Fabri (Köckritz) Sabothus, p. 16. Lips. 1715. 8.*

'Aldabaron, called by the Hebrews Luz.' [III.iii.451]*

As this antiquity in osteological history seems to have been banished from anatomical works since the good old days of Bartholinus and Kulmus, it will perhaps be agreeable to the curious reader to find here some notice of it, collected out of the rabbinical writings, &c. by the author's Russian friend Bernhard Reich, whose knowledge of the science and the language necessary renders him singularly capable of such investigations.

The bone Luz (לוז) is, according to the Rabbins, the only one which withstands dissolution after death, out of which the body will be developed at the resurrection. A curious passage on the subject occurs in Bereshith raba. Sect. 28, של שדרה שממנו הק'בה מציץ את האדם לעתיד לבא נמחה אפילו לוז 'Even the Luz of the shedrah, שדרה (*backbone*) out of which God will hereafter raise the son of earth, is annihilated'. Old anatomists as Bartholinus, Vesalius, &c. mention it, but are not certain what bone was so designated, whether it is situated in the hand, foot, or vertebral column; Luz לוז is however beyond a doubt the os coccygis of the osteologians, for the rabbins say that it lies under the eighteenth Chulia חוליא *vertebra*. (Maaroch Hamarachot Article לוז), and it appears from various passages in the Talmud that the vertebræ of the neck were not reckoned by the rabbinical writers to the vertebral column שדרה, but that they began to count the latter from the first dorsal vertebra, like Hippocrates (de ossium naturâ, V.) They say בשדרה י״ח עוליות 18 vertebræ (*chuliot*) compose the shedrah שדרה vertebral column — See Ohol. c. I. Berach p. 30. Now, if we reckon the twelve dorsal, five lumbal, vertebræ, and the os sacrum together, we have the eighteen bones under which Luz is to be found: Luz is therefore the os coccygis. Etymology is also for this opinion; for Luz לוז is an almond; the Targum Jonathan translates in many places the Hebrew Shaked שקד almond, plural Sheᵉkedim שקדים Luz and Luzin לוז, לוזיו (Num. 17. 23, &c.). The form of the bone is really similar to that of an almond. In the lexicon we find the explanation of the word given from κόκκυξ, cuckoo, but this bird appears to have very little to do with the bone, and it is probable that the term is derived by some corruption from κόκκος, a nut or the seed of any tree. Mr. Reich to whom I am obliged for the above intends to publish shortly an academical disquisition on the subject, which, enriched as it will be, with many very ingenious suppositions and curious discussions on the philosophy and language of the Jews and other orientals, will form a very acceptable Essay towards the history of the remarkable doctrine of the resurrection, and many other points of Judaical physiology & religion.

EDITORIAL NOTES

'Preface' (p. 3): Beddoes's preface had no heading in Dykes Campbell's 'MS. II'.

Bilderdijk (p. 4): Donner identifies and quotes the passage from Bilderdijk's essay, but it was not transcribed by Campbell (see *Works*, pp. 714–15).

'a German critic just mentioned' (p. 5): A.W. Schlegel, from whom Beddoes adapts the analogy between an English tragedy and a Gothic cathedral.

'a living writer who will occur to the reader' (p. 6): Donner suggests that this is intended as a (rather extravagant) compliment to Procter (*Works*, p. 715).

Greek epigraph (p. 9): '[The motto] refers to Archedemos, the alien politician whom the Athenians disliked, but who, according to Aristophanes, was demagogue among the dead and contrived to keep the leadership in that "rascaldom". — "Let us haste to the meadows where they hold their vigil, let us haste to the roses in those meadows in our own old fashion."' (From Donner's note, *Works*, p. 712).

'The historical fact...' (p. 122): Beddoes's note refers to Karl Friedrich Flögel, *Geschichte der Hofnarren* (1789). The Latin quotation can be roughly translated: 'So after the Fool [*Morio*], provoked by chance, had extinguished the Bolco line by sharply throwing a brick (which was considered at that time an omen of the destruction of the nation) at the last heir, the dynasty became sterile and thus there was no hope at the Court.'

'Aldabaron, called by the Hebrews Luz' (p. 122): The account of Jewish doctrine here is well researched, although Reich seems never to have published his treatise. For further discussion of Beddoes's relationship with Jewish doctrine, see Christopher Moylan, '"For Luz is a Good Joke": Thomas Lovell Beddoes and Jewish Eschatology' (2002), listed in the bibliography.

THOMAS LOVELL BEDDOES SOCIETY

The Thomas Lovell Beddoes Society was set up in 1994 to encourage a revival of interest in this powerful but unjustly neglected English poet and other members of his remarkable family, such as his father, the physician and scientist Dr Thomas Beddoes, and his aunt, the novelist Maria Edgeworth. The Society also acts as a focus for Beddoes family history.

The Society is a member of the Alliance of Literary Societies. It issues an annual Newsletter and a number of booklets, mostly of literary criticism, on Beddoes-related topics and has produced a tape-recording of readings from Beddoes's poetry. Its Annual General Meeting is held in a place with Beddoes connections, differing from year to year, and usually takes the form of a residential weekend with informal lectures and guided walks.

The Society welcomes new members, both individual and institutional. A leaflet (also available in German) giving further information can be obtained from:

John Lovell Beddoes
11 Laund Nook
Belper
Derbyshire
DE56 1GY
UK

or consult the Society's website at
http://www.beddoes.demon.co.uk

Patrons
Kevin Crossley-Holland FRSL
Patrick Leigh Fermor DSO, OBE
Professor James R. Thompson

Charity No. 1041402

FyfieldBooks

Two millennia of essential classics

The extensive Fyfield*Books* list includes

Djuna Barnes *The Book of Repulsive Women and other poems*
edited by Rebecca Loncraine

Elizabeth Barrett Browning *Selected Poems* edited by Malcolm Hicks

Charles Baudelaire *Complete Poems in French and English*
translated by Walter Martin

The Brontë Sisters *Selected Poems*
edited by Stevie Davies

Lewis Carroll *Selected Poems*
edited by Keith Silver

Thomas Chatterton *Selected Poems*
edited by Grevel Lindop

John Clare *By Himself*
edited by Eric Robinson and David Powell

Samuel Taylor Coleridge *Selected Poetry* edited by William Empson and David Pirie

John Donne *Selected Letters*
edited by P.M. Oliver

Oliver Goldsmith *Selected Writings*
edited by John Lucas

Victor Hugo *Selected Poetry in French and English*
translated by Steven Monte

Wyndham Lewis *Collected Poems and Plays* edited by Alan Munton

Charles Lamb *Selected Writings*
edited by J.E. Morpurgo

Ben Jonson *Epigrams and The Forest*
edited by Richard Dutton

Giacomo Leopardi *The Canti*
with a selection of his prose
translated by J.G. Nichols

Andrew Marvell *Selected Poems*
edited by Bill Hutchings

Charlotte Mew *Collected Poems and Selected Prose*
edited by Val Warner

Michelangelo *Sonnets*
translated by Elizabeth Jennings,
introduction by Michael Ayrton

William Morris *Selected Poems*
edited by Peter Faulkner

Ovid *Amores*
translated by Tom Bishop

Edgar Allan Poe *Poems and Essays on Poetry*
edited by C.H. Sisson

Restoration Bawdy
edited by John Adlard

Rainer Maria Rilke *Sonnets to Orpheus and Letters to a Young Poet*
translated by Stephen Cohn

Christina Rossetti *Selected Poems*
edited by C.H. Sisson

Sir Walter Scott *Selected Poems*
edited by James Reed

Sir Philip Sidney *Selected Writings*
edited by Richard Dutton

Henry Howard, Earl of Surrey *Selected Poems*
edited by Dennis Keene

Algernon Charles Swinburne *Selected Poems*
edited by L.M. Findlay

Oscar Wilde *Selected Poems*
edited by Malcolm Hicks

Sir Thomas Wyatt *Selected Poems*
edited by Hardiman Scott

For more information, including a full list of Fyfield*Books* and a contents list for each title, and details of how to order the books in the UK, visit the Fyfield website at www.fyfieldbooks.co.uk or email info@fyfieldbooks.co.uk. For information about Fyfield*Books* available in the United States and Canada, visit the Routledge website at www.routledge-ny.com.